THE HOUSE ON MASONIC

A Haight-Ashbury Story

A NOVEL BY

SUSAN KNAPP

LUMINARE PRESS

WWW.LUMINAREPRESS.COM

The House on Masonic: A Haight-Ashbury Story
© 2017 Susan Knapp

Printed in the United States of America

Cover illustration by Susan Knapp
Cover design by Claire Flint Last

Luminare Press
438 Charnelton St., Suite 101
Eugene, OR 97401
www.luminarepress.com

LCCN: 2017941801
ISBN: 978-1-944733-31-5

To Peter Szasz, my friend and
my brother in all but blood.

1941-2017

You saved my bacon more than once, sat with me
through a bad trip, fed me, gave me a place to crash,
made me laugh when things were tough, and helped me
when it was time to leave the Haight.

You were a good soul (even if you did love puns).

Rest in peace.

ACKNOWLEDGMENTS

Many thanks to my Beta Readers and commentators:

Kathy Brandon, Cindy Glaser, Carolyn McDonald, Joan Oppel, and Susan Vaughn. Each of them brought a unique perspective to that task and their proofing, comments, and personal memories of the 60s helped to make this a better book.

A special thanks also goes out, once again, to my friends in Ashland who have supported me so much in all my writing efforts. And, finally, as always, I am forever grateful to my colleagues at Luminare Press who have brought their talents and expertise to bear in putting this book together.

PROLOGUE

San Francisco, Potrero Hill, 1970

I dug out my "time capsule" this morning, an old cedar chest where I've put things from my "hippie days." Maybe I'll keep collecting until it's full. And then, lock it up and turn it into a coffee table or something. I tell myself I want to save it all for the next generation or for my old age when I need stuff to jog my memory.

I've made a list of the contents. (I'm famous for my lists, and they're all over the place: to-do lists, birthday lists, shopping lists, all my addresses in San Francisco, etc.) I suppose it's my way of creating order out of chaos. Anyway…

Contents:
- My old derby with its pink daisy
- A madras wall hanging
- Three copies of the *Oracle*
- Two issues of the Sunday *San Francisco Chronicle* paper, complete with ads
- Five concert flyers and a few posters from the Fillmore
- Two packets of Zig-Zag rolling papers
- A recipe for grass brownies
- Sandalwood stick incense
- A cool roach clip: an alligator clip attached with copper wire to an ornate silver-plated knife handle
- Hippie beads
- A list of my acid trips
- Etc.

(I'm trying to reform, to say things like "etc." rather than including every damn item.)

The only things I haven't been able to get are Zander's draft card and army discharge papers. He says he wants to keep proof of his medical discharge handy. I can't very well blame him; the war isn't over, after all.

I started making the collection last year when I read an article in the *Chronicle* about an archeological dig they were doing near the wharf. Seems there was a printer down there before the earthquake, in the late 1890's. For some reason, the researchers were really puzzled about the ink he used. Good stuff and they had no idea what the formula was. If it was ever written down, there was no record of it now.

It made me think. That was only 60 or maybe 70 years ago and already things were forgotten. Things come and go, and it's easy to lose them forever. Hell, we even forget that we've forgotten stuff all the time.

Like, if I hadn't been thinking about the time capsule, would I have remembered this afternoon that when I was twelve, I didn't think I'd live beyond eighteen?

Kinda morbid for a kid, but that's the way it was with me.

Partly, it was my youth and a failure of imagination; still, in some respects I think I was right. After all, at eighteen, I spent my first four days at college alone in my new dorm room, only leaving to get packs of peanut butter crackers from a vending machine. Those four days felt like a very long time, but eventually my roomie arrived, and I started classes and a new life.

When I was twelve, we lived in a suburb of Chicago. It was the post-war (WWII) world and lots of us had those houses they put up in big suburban subdivisions that were all alike. Oh, the floor plan might get flipped from one to another, and the colors might be different (as long as they were white, tan, or gray), but that was it. We all had one maple or oak tree sapling out front to grow up with the two or three kids inside.

We all went to the same schools, our moms all had their hair done at the same place, and they shopped at the same stores. I guess it's not surprising we all looked pretty similar. Oh, and of course, everyone was pretty much white and Christian. We ate the same foods at home or school, and we were all middle-class and upwardly mobile. On television, we watched sitcoms featuring families just like ours (*Father Knows Best* and *Leave it to Beaver*, for example), and all the magazines and their advertising were aimed at us.

Everyone was happy, at least on the outside. We knew from television and magazines what a happy family should look like, and we kept up appearances. I guess the inside didn't matter, although sometimes I wonder now what it was like to watch those shows if you were an immigrant in the city or weren't white.

By the time the 60s rolled around, I think that way of life had started to get a bit stale for our parents. They certainly were drinking too much and too often. Everyone had a bar in their basement rec rooms for parties and cocktail hours. And, of course, everyone smoked lots of cigarettes.

Products of the Great Depression and war years, this was the life my parents had dreamed of, but they didn't seem very happy. Not that they said anything.

As for us kids, well, we weren't exactly entranced by the life of grownups. It seemed kind of empty. Too many fake smiles, too much hypocrisy, and too many things you couldn't talk about – like sex and money. Nobody ever talked about what things cost or how much they made. (Money was almost as bad as sex and shame was involved with both. At least, that's the way it seemed.)

When I reached puberty, my mother gave me a book: *Being Born*. Maybe I was dumb; I didn't get it. Not surprising really: it dealt with pregnancy more than how you got that way. It didn't seem to have anything to do with "love" or the word no one ever said ("sex") and the relationships between them was really fuzzy.

Somehow, it was clear to me that whatever was going on was scary, and as I got a little older, I got more uncomfortable with any kind of big feelings. I didn't want to care; I didn't want to feel. I was most comfortable sitting back in my head and being an observer or maybe a bit player in someone else's movie. (I wasn't good enough for a starring role.)

My parents sent me to a counselor of some sort at one point. They hadn't asked me about going, so I refused to talk. For two sessions, I sat and stared at the clock on the wall until my time was up. That was the end of that.

Sometimes, I thought that I felt the emptiness of my life more acutely than my brother did because I was a girl. He had options for a future, while all I had was wife/mother, teacher, nurse, secretary, and… nothing else came to mind.

I couldn't be a veterinarian. I wasn't strong enough to birth a cow, so that idea got shot down fast by my school guidance counselor. Going to college was good, yes. After all, what better place to find the ambitious young men? But, women couldn't have careers. Not really, or only rarely. Very rarely. It was also clear that having a career was the fall back for the woman who couldn't find a man. As if that wasn't enough, "career" women were suspect people that I was supposed to be wary of for some reason.

Boys were privileged and had more options, sure, but

it wasn't like they had any real role models either. Where was the adventure? How could they be creative? What about excitement, maybe even a bit of danger? How could they be a "Man" if they were stuck in an office pushing papers around their desks like their Dads? (Who knows – maybe the Dads wondered, too.)

We all wanted to do something, and we wanted to feel lots of things, too, but it was just so confusing sometimes.

Our parents weren't much help. After all, we were still asking "why" long after children were supposed to have outgrown that. It was amazing enough we asked the questions; our parents didn't want to even think about the answers. I mean, what on earth could they say? We were obviously not buying any of it.

The James Dean movie, *Rebel without a Cause*, sure stirred things up. And what about Brando on his motorcycle! Not exactly the role models they'd hoped for.

At least the boys had guys like them to emulate; girls didn't have anybody. Who could we look to? The ones who ran after the boys and movie stars? Bobbysoxers and swooning teens, the party goers, the "fast" ones?

Sure, a few movie stars like Katherine Hepburn played career girls, but she was so much older. Historical figures like Madame Curie? Yeah, but she was even older and foreign. Some singers…but what if you didn't have a voice?

My mother kept saying I was a "late bloomer." She thought I'd find my way when I got a little older or something. Not helpful, especially since every time she said that I'd picture an old bouquet of roses with sad, brown buds that never bloomed.

I guess it's no wonder I didn't think I'd have much of a life after 18.

I went away to college, as expected, but stopped going to classes my junior year and drifted to San Francisco in 1962.

I would never have predicted that.

BOOK ONE

Turn On, Tune In, Drop Out

(February to April, 1967)

CHAPTER ONE

San Francisco in 1967 had an unreal glamour about it – in the old sense of the word: a magic spell. Of course, everyone was drunk or stoned and all our perceptions were probably skewed, but still, the very sky felt heavy with meaning. People, events, inanimate objects – they all took on "significance." I wasn't always sure what the significance was; I just knew it all meant something important.

And weird things kept happening. Like that day when I was walking to work at the diner, thinking about I don't know what, and I happened to glance up at a house I was passing. It was just another of the ubiquitous Victorians with wide front steps and a deep stoop, but I did a double-take that almost gave me whiplash: there was a big lion up there. Not a concrete sculpture – a real, live lion! He was sitting there, as if it was…I don't know…Africa? A library? He was huge, tawny, and disturbingly alert.

A couple of guys walked out the door and the one with long hair put a leash on the big cat while they talked.

A leash? Really? That was going to be worth anything?

I kept on walking, trying to be cool, you know, and not making any sudden movements. I didn't relax until I turned the corner; then I laughed.

Well, it was San Francisco, I thought. Anything was obviously possible here. That, at least, was hopeful.

February: No more school for me. I now had all the credits I needed for my BA in English Lit. I wouldn't get my diploma until June when they did the graduation ceremonies, but I wouldn't go to that. It wasn't like I was really part of the SF State Class of '67. If I'd stayed at Northwestern and the people I met there my freshman year, maybe then I would have gone. But, dropping out like I did, no.

That always sounded more active than it was: "dropping out." I just stopped going to classes and didn't bother with the paper work. Not sure why; I just couldn't muster the energy for it.

Mom was disappointed and Dad was pretty pissed. (He thought he'd wasted a lot of money on nothing and that college should just be for boys, like my baby brother. He thought I should have gone to secretarial school and learned shorthand. Shorthand: that was the last thing I wanted to do. I knew that much.)

It took the school a couple of months to kick me out of the dorms as a non-student, and then Dee, a classmate who was transferring to Stanford, was driving west so I tagged along with her. I ended up getting a job in San Francisco, in The City, aka Baghdad by the Bay, as it was variously called. I established residency and after a year I went back to school. At $49 per semester, I could afford to work my way through college, taking whatever courses I wanted and loosely aiming for my BA.

Some semesters I worked full time, went to school part-time; others, I'd switch. Mostly I worked in financial district clerical jobs and went to school. After work, I'd study, write papers, let the guys at the corner bar buy me a drink, read, and go to bed. That was my life; that and moving around. By the time I finished my degree, I'd moved ten times. Sometimes I had roomies, others I lived alone, and a couple of times I had summer live-in "mother's helper" jobs. I think I sometimes just got tired of living where I was and wanted a change.

Anyway, with all that, it took me five years to get through what would have been my junior and senior years, so no, I didn't really identify with any particular "class."

Was that really all of my life? Well, other than school… once a week I played chess and drank a bottle of Guinness with my old friend Zander. We'd been classmates at Northwestern, and I ran into him at the streetcar stop at Market and Castro a couple of years ago. Pretty cool; I was really glad to see him. Besides chess, we'd also started to go ice skating at Sutro's over on the coast.

Oh, yes, and lest I dare to forget – every once in a while I used to have a meal and/or get drunk with Gwen and Liz: my "disturbing friends." Some friends they were – I had hopes it was finally over between us. But enough of that; what was I going to do now? Go to grad school? Maybe, but it would be all literary criticism now, which wasn't very appealing. I mean I liked reading the books, not taking them apart.

Maybe I was finally done with school? I could look for a better job, but I still had one, even if it was only slinging hash at the diner three blocks away. Cool, for what it was, and certainly better than working downtown at an insurance company or bank. No bus fare needed and no business attire required, only a uniform, the white nylon dress I washed out every night. Best part of the deal: I got to eat for free anytime I went in, not just when I was working. Saved a lot of money that way.

So, no school for now, and when I wasn't working I had

big, empty stretches of time. I felt…what? I don't know; I just wanted to crawl back under the covers and pull them over my head in the mornings. Everything felt "off" somehow. Certainly I was.

If I got desperate, I had a couple of casual friends, I could have coffee or a beer with, and, if I got really, really desperate, there were those problematic, difficult…No, we weren't talking again, and that was fine with me, no matter how desperate I got. I just hoped the estrangement would last this time.

Zander was my best friend, and I'd really missed him during his a brief stint with the army. They'd drafted him even with his bum knee. When it swelled up like a melon during basic training, they dumped him before they had to pay for all his medical bills.

These days he had a full time job, his painting, and a new girlfriend. Talk about settling back in to civilian life! Anyway, he didn't have much time for anything else, unless he was fighting with his girlfriend, which happened with some regularity.

I wasn't sure what they fought about, but it wasn't what they said it was. More like when married couples argue about money and there's really something else going on.

CHAPTER TWO

Spring, 1967 and it was raining. Again.

A whole lot of rain that year. The only time it had cleared up a little was in January when they had the gathering they called the "Human Be-In" in Golden Gate Park. The sun made a short appearance and then left when the whole thing was over. I didn't go (crowds spook me) so I just read about it in the paper. It was some sort of celebration; I wasn't clear at the time what it was all about.

After that, the monsoons returned and kept hanging on. And on. At least the weather matched my mood: cold, dreary, cloudy, and wet.

I had a tall stack of books I'd been saving for "when I graduated," and now that I had a ton of time, I couldn't seem to sit still long enough to read more than a couple of paragraphs. Nothing grabbed me.

That had never happened before. I'd always been an obsessive reader.

Kinda spooked me a little, to tell the truth.

So, I went off to work at the diner, put in my time, closed up if I was working the evening shift, and came home to wash out my uniform. Sometimes I managed to type a few lines in my journal on the old Underwood. Maybe I'd listen to the radio for a while. No TV...I couldn't afford one. Too bad, maybe it would have helped, provided a distraction from the crummy tape loop in my head that kept telling me what a miserable loser I was. Bad enough that it was true.

I mean, who did I think I was, anyway?

I was Miss Average.

Average height, average weight, medium brown hair.

Blah.

Meaning invisible, ignorable, and forgettable.

Zander turned me on to the *I Ching* that spring, an ancient Chinese book of divinations he'd heard about. I think the big selling point for him was the introduction by Jung. The artist in him really related to all the pages on Jung's work with archetypes.

The first time I sat down with the *I Ching* I asked it what I was doing, where I was going. I threw the three coins six times to create a hexagram and got "The Wanderer" and being a "stranger in a strange land."

I sure felt like that a lot. It was also the title of a favorite Heinlein book of mine. Was it a coincidence? Seemed unlikely. Was it important? Meaningful beyond the words some way? Seemed like it should be, but who knew?

I did know that I needed more guidance than the *I Ching* provided. I'd already tried therapy; what else could I explore? Astrology was certainly very "in." Hell, I couldn't walk down the street without someone asking what my sign was. So, I learned how to do horoscopes. It turned out I was an Aries with a Taurus rising and a Moon in Taurus. That explained a lot of things about me which weren't typically Aries.

Not that I really believed in astrology. I was only playing around with it. I found it a better language to describe people than the Freudian stuff my problematic friends liked. I mean, it was so much nicer to say a person had heavy

Capricorn influences than that they were anal retentive.

Besides, I liked all the diagrams and calculations. Sort of like making lists.

Anyway, it was fun, and I didn't want to get real deeply into it. I wanted to keep it light, not get all heavy or anything.

CHAPTER THREE

One night I decided to take a break from astrology, from feeling bad about my life, and not reading. There was a revival of *A Hard Day's Night* at the movie theater around the corner. I hadn't seen it when it first came out, dismissing all the hoopla. I mean the Beatles were just another rock band, right? Doo-wop and all that?

Well, I had to change my mind: those guys were different and crazy funny. The music certainly wasn't the rock n' roll I was used to and didn't particularly like. The music these boys played was…well, far out, as they liked to say. And, they were so irreverent! Oh, I really loved that.

They mocked the establishment by showing its absurdities and got everyone to laugh with them. Playfully, not with anger, not like the folks over in Berkeley. Those folks seemed to be pissed all the time, and they were so damn serious and, worse, self-righteous.

The Beatles were so cool that I started paying more attention to what was happening in the Haight. I'd heard stories on the streets, at the streetcar stop, and, of course, in the newspapers about the kids there, "hippies" they called them. A little scary to a lot of people because of their differences and their casual disregard for convention. Personally, I found them intriguing and, yeah, a little attractive. I sort of wanted to be like them, at least in some ways, but I didn't have the nerve.

I knew it wasn't all "sex, drugs, and rock and roll," in

spite of what the papers said. It was interesting that when they were organizing the Human Be-In, the hippies and the Berkeley radicals tried to make common cause. That must have been something. They did agree about not wanting any part of the established institutions, capitalism, wars, etc. They had a fair amount in common; the main problem seemed to be in what to do with it.

Like, when the Berkeley people heard the Be-In would attract maybe fifty thousand people, they wanted to draw up a long list of demands, and the Haight-Ashbury community thought that was ridiculous. They thought the Be-In was a celebration, an opportunity to "be," to come together.

Even when they were trying to be tolerant of one another, I could tell there was condescension on both sides. Lots of head shaking and "Can you believe that cat?" kind of thing. Each side was "right" and all the others "wrong" if you dug down deep enough. And, each thought they were the central hub for whatever was happening, and everybody else was peripheral and basically unimportant. It wasn't just the Berkeley folks and the Haight people who felt that way. The guys who called themselves "Diggers," the Hells Angels, Black Panthers, Free Speech Movement folks, and the Weathermen – they all had their own things going on, and, of course, the Krishnas, and…well, the list seemed to go on forever and didn't even include the Vietnam War hawks and doves, the Birchers, the Socialists, etc. (And, in San Francisco, we even had Satanists!)

Near as I could tell some people wanted to wage war against war and everything else, while others wanted to wage peace. (I wasn't sure what that entailed besides making peace hand signs and saying, "Peace and love, brother. Peace and love.") Still, something must have been working right for the hippies to get the Hells Angels (of all people) to feel mellow and protective of them.

I've never much cared for politics and politicians of whatever stripe, but among all those groups were people who were thinking, feeling, and wondering about the powers of the mind and the heart. For all my cynicism, they interested me. They talked about how to live and relate to/ with one another, and I heard a lot of stuff about slowing down, being in the now, simplifying life, being gentle and loving, turning on, and dropping out. I wasn't sure what they were talking about lots of times, but I listened.

The summer I worked at the post office as a mail sorter some of the mail carriers were hippies. I enjoyed their spirit, and there were rumors that after they picked up their bags of mail, everyone in their commune would come down to help make the deliveries. They'd finish in a couple of hours, so the customers got their mail along with the morning paper.

I liked the idea of shaking up the post office bureaucracy, being imaginative, cooperative, and, at the same time, more efficient. Very cool.

Of course, the post office didn't much care for it and fired them when they figured out what was going on. The hippies didn't seem bothered. They had each other and a certain conviction that everything would turn out all right. The universe would provide. Wow, I thought it must be cool to have such faith.

All last fall, when I took the streetcar down to the financial district, I could see how day by day the hair was growing longer and longer on lots of people in my regular crowd on the streetcars. Nehru jackets appeared along with bell-bottoms, beads, head bands, and paisley patterns. Certainly not the financial district uniform of a year or two ago, and a far cry from the 50s when we all dressed alike in our crew-neck sweaters, straight skirts, and penny loafers.

The 50s were a predictable, regimented era. These new people were something else and I envied their ease and beauty, and okay, yes, I loved the costumes, too. Dressing up...it was a little like Halloween all the time.

I found a pair of tall black boots at Goodwill and purple cords I could tuck in the boots. I already had a pea coat, so that was taken care of. I finished off the outfit with a courier bag I made from an old tan cash bag with a Wells Fargo stencil I found. All I had to do was sew on leather straps and I had something cool for all my stuff.

Zander gave me a derby for my birthday and I stuck a fabric daisy in the hat band. A pair of wire rim sun glasses and some beaded necklaces finished things off. (I made the beads myself.)

I wasn't a hippie, but I was starting to look a little like one in my off hours.

The girls across the hall had turned me on to the new DJ who was playing lots of Beach Boys stuff as well as The Beatles, Doors, and Jefferson Airplane. I still liked Joan Baez and Barbra Streisand, but the new music hit me in a different place, challenged me in a way the old stuff didn't. Okay, yes, the Beach Boys' lyrics were pretty sappy, but the music and harmonies...man, they blew me away.

If only I knew more about music, I could describe it better. Maybe it was just as well I didn't; I'd started to see that words might not be the key to life. Not mine, in any case,

Actually, I thought words might be more of a cage.

I wasn't sure what that meant, but it felt true.

CHAPTER FOUR

After I finished with my course work, I continued working at the diner and the days drifted by. At night I sat in my little apartment, smoked cigarettes, drank beer and wine, and listened to the radio. I still couldn't read – I'd pick up a book and my eyes would slide away, around, up, down. I might as well have been drunk, but I wasn't. Not always, anyway. So, no reading, and I wasn't sleeping well either. I had trouble falling asleep and then woke up at 3:30 or 4:00 in the morning, no matter what time I went to bed. At least I could still write a little. I'd break out my old black Underwood and type away. There was something almost cheery in the "ding" at the end of a line. Almost.

Sun, rain, sleep, insomnia, it didn't make much difference. I was bleak.

A good word: "bleak." Made me think of dark, cloudy moors and Bronte novels.

The question of the day: What was next for me?

I didn't have a clue and the *I Ching* wasn't being helpful. I did know, at least, that I was tired of letting the DJs pick my music all the time. I wanted to listen to the music I wanted to listen to when I wanted, so I scraped up a couple of bucks to buy a little portable stereo to supplement my radio.

Then, of course, I needed to try it out to see if it worked

and figure out what albums to buy.

I'd heard the music coming from the apartment across the hall and seen the two girls who lived there start to change over the last few months, getting more hippie-like each week. Pam, the quiet, somewhat shy one, now had long, straight dark hair held back with a beaded Indian headband, while Sandra, the one with a lot of nervous energy, couldn't do much with her red curly hair and pulled it back in a leather clasp to keep it out of the way. Cute girls and very young.

Lately, I'd noticed a few more people living there and the music played almost constantly. I told myself it would be okay to ask if they'd lend me an album. The girls always nodded to me in passing, and we knew each other's names and all.

When I knocked, a young guy with long dark hair and a full beard answered the door by peeking around the edge at me. He looked a little freaked out to see me; I think it was the white uniform.

"Hi," I said. "I'm Terry Walker. I live across the hall," and I gestured vaguely over my shoulder. "I just got a new stereo and wondered if I could borrow an album to try it out."

"Oh, sure, that'll probably be okay." He let the door open more widely, and Sandra stuck her head around the corner from the kitchen.

"She's cool, Mike. Our neighbor...Want some soup?" she asked me.

I said I had to go to work in a little while and she went back to stirring a pot, while Mike started looking through the stacks of albums lined up around the walls on the floor.

Pretty much everything was on the floor: beds, cushions, albums, record player, speakers. Over in one corner a new girl was sitting cross legged on a mattress. Very much a California blue-eyed blonde, a surfer/hippie chick with bare feet. She didn't look too good, and I gathered she was sick.

"Hey, Sandra, what about lending her this Buffalo Springfield?" called Mike.

Sandra abandoned the kitchen. "Let me see; it might be Pam's. Nope; it's mine. Sure, you can borrow it."

Mike was lighting up a joint by this time and offered me a toke. A bit of a test, I thought. Like was I a narc or something? So, I said thanks and took a hit. Not the first time for me, but I hadn't smoked a lot.

I'd been feeling a bit funny and out of place, in my uniform and all, but after that, things got noticeably more relaxed, and I didn't think it was just the grass. I got introduced to the girl on the mattress (Sunny) and a guy who'd been hiding out in the kitchen (he had some odd Indian name, I think).

Sandra told me that Pam had hitchhiked down to Santa Cruz for the weekend. By herself, I gathered, and they all seemed to think it was safe for her to do that. I'd always been taught hitchhiking was in the same camp as taking candy from strangers: really dumb for a girl to do. Maybe things had changed…or they were crazy.

I took the album and left with an open invitation to drop by anytime.

I hate to admit it, but I felt a little like I'd received an invitation to join the cool kids at their school lunch table. Real hippies. Especially Sunny. They said she even knew Timothy Leary and assorted rockers. Celebrities. I was impressed.

I liked them. I especially liked their openness and easiness. I was so dark, and they were so light and free and different from me.

I started hanging around, buying a bit of grass from them, bringing over groceries, and sitting and talking with Sunny as she recuperated from mono.

To pass the time as she regained her strength, she drew. She'd sit down with a black pen that had a very fine point and make intricate, abstract designs. Then she colored in the spaces with vibrant colored inks in red, green, violet, orange, etc. They were beautiful in their own way, and I was as intrigued by the process, her dedicated attention and careful, precise pen strokes, as much as I was with the end products.

While she worked, she talked about her little boy, Joey, who lived with her parents back in Ohio. Then she went on to talk about guys she'd met, like Leary, Metzner, and Kesey. She'd been a band groupie, traveled across the country, and taken a lot of LSD. Many stories about lots of adventures.

I spent a fair amount of time over there. I'd go over after I got home from work, and Sunny and I would sit around the kitchen table and talk. We were both a little older than the others and had that in common.

We smoked grass together, and she smiled a great deal. Her smile…it was so open and full of joy, pleasure, and delight. You wanted to see it again, to make her smile, to have her smile at you.

She believed in loving everybody, she said, and, by God, it really seemed she did. It blew my mind. I loved that in her, as well as her faith in the dawning of the Age of Aquarius. She said everything was going to change for the better when that happened, and I wanted to believe it.

I had to admit that I did think she might be a little nuts,

too, but I didn't care. It was all beautiful and I enjoyed being around her.

She told me the story of her life, and I didn't know if I believed it all or not. Pretty outrageous stuff, like something out of a Steinbeck novel or a TV soap opera.

Her dead father had been a bouncer and a bootlegger. She and her mother lived in a trailer park when she was growing up, and I guess her dad had died or something, because then her mother went through lots of other men until she married again and they moved to the burbs.

Sunny was pretty wild herself – a high school kid going to drinking parties, getting knocked up and having a kid. She was a runaway at one point and the principle found her and begged her to come back to school and get her diploma. Later, she was at Ohio State, but she dropped out when she discovered that the groovy guy who worked in the book store was really a narc.

There was time in a loony bin and shock treatments, too, but I wasn't clear exactly when. Anyway, when she reached eighteen, her new stepfather kicked her out. He put her suitcase on the doorstep and changed the locks.

He did leave an envelope for her with $40 and a note saying they'd keep Joey until she got her act together. Still, pretty hard; I couldn't imagine what that was like. Sort of like being thrown out of a plane, I guessed. Not having her kid was tough for her, but she knew she'd have more luck getting a permanent place for him and so forth if she didn't have to worry about day care while she looked.

After that, she started wandering around and found Leary and his bunch in upstate New York. Then, a couple of months ago, a seer had given her a tarot card reading saying she would go west to a city by the water where she would find everything she wanted. So, she left and hitched to San Francisco.

Everybody still called it "Sunny San Francisco," after all – even if it had been raining a lot lately. The City's nickname was a sign for Sunny, a directional message. So she headed this way.

Soon after she arrived, she fell in with a young, rich guy, Jason, who owned a music store and was a rock band promoter and producer. He was, she told me, a great man and a gentle, evolved soul. She'd always been looking for "The Man," it seemed, and he was the one. I wasn't sure what that was…part guru, part he-man, part artist? I wasn't really clear. She said she thought it was important he was another Aquarius, like her, and maybe she wanted somebody who would help her get her kid back. I knew she wanted to have a real family someday.

Anyway, although she thought Jason was her guy, things had gotten ugly lately. He'd started hitting her, and then he kicked her out. (Didn't sound much like the act of a "gentle soul" to me, but I kept my mouth shut.)

After she came down with mono, friends moved her in here to recuperate.

She was only twenty-four.

Jesus. Two years younger than me and, looking at my life in suburbia, my family…what could I say to her about myself? Not much. I was just the usual 50s kid stuck in a comfortable cage in which nothing much seemed to happen.

I summed up my life for her in a couple of sentences and that was all I had.

CHAPTER FIVE

We talked and smoked a lot of grass those first weeks while Sunny recuperated. I had a lot of questions, and she was happy to answer them. Like, there were so many names for marihuana – pot, grass, weed, reefer, dope, etc. – were they for different drugs or the same? I wasn't clear.

Mostly all the same thing, she said, but "reefer" was usually just another term for marihuana rolled into a joint. There were also specific names for some marihuana depending on their origin (like Acapulco Gold or Jamaican Red) or specific preparation, like "ganja," which was all flowers and tips and might or might not be Jamaican.

She reassured me that there wasn't a "right" term. People on the east coast said one thing, people down in LA another. Ditto for African-Americans from Harlem or the Caribbean, Mexicans, etc. Right here, right now, "grass" and "weed" seemed to be the most common terms. At least as far as she could tell.

What about "straights" and "squares" for the mainstream people? Hippies, she explained, mostly distinguished between themselves and the "straights" – people who never got high, took any of the psychedelic drugs, and got their consciousness expanded. "Square" on the other hand was a little left-over term for the older folks who didn't like rock n' roll music. At least that was her impression; she couldn't say for sure.

Made some sense to me and I liked getting all that sorted out.

I was curious about the psychedelics, and I watched Sunny as she took LSD ("acid"). She offered me some, but I was reluctant to try it. Strong stuff and sometimes people had a bad time on it. I was intrigued, sure, but I wasn't ready to drop acid, "drop out," or quit my job, and I had a feeling they all sort of went together.

It wasn't like job titles and money had ever been much of a motivator for me. Maybe that was because I grew up with enough money and stuff. And, since I'd dropped out of school and bummed around, I'd worked all sorts of jobs, lived in basements, slept on floors, and eaten spaghetti with a ketchup sauce for dinner. I liked my comforts, sure, but at the same time, I wasn't afraid of roughing it. I was cool with all that, but I suspected there was more to it.

When I watched Sunny and the others take acid, I saw a light in them, and there wasn't any in my soul. I wondered if acid could save me from the darkness inside. Show me a way out?

Sunny thought so; I wasn't so sure.

Anyway…while I thought about it, I tried to make myself useful bringing them groceries and fixing a few things.

I always liked being handy. It was fun for me and, considering my income, a practical talent. I kept a twenty inch long cardboard box in my closet filled with supplies I'd put together over the years from stuff I'd found in trash heaps, in the Good Will bins, or at the curb on trash day. Amazing what people will throw away and how easy it is to fix a lamp and lots of other broken things.

What did my neighbors need? Well, a light switch wasn't

working and I replaced it, and the second screw on a cabinet handle had disappeared and I found one to substitute. Nothing major, little stuff I could feel good doing, and they were appreciative.

Pam brought home a couple of rich boys from Texas who started hanging around. They had money, good cars with leather seats and tape decks, and the assurance daddy in Dallas would take care of them. That sounds obnoxious, but actually they were really rather sweet and sort of innocent. One of them scored a bunch of acid to take back to Texas, and he gave me a tab to take, a blue dot on a Vitamin C tab. (Sunny told me the first acid should always be free and I should tuck it away for when I was ready.)

Somewhere in there, Dee, that old classmate of mine who'd driven me across country and was now living in LA, decided to come up and stay with me for a couple of days. I'd written her about my neighbors, and she wasn't too sure about Sunny, how real she was and how good for me she might or might not be. I thought it was nice of her to look out for me, but didn't think it was necessary.

It got kind of crowded. Thank God, the Texas boys were staying in a hotel. Could have been worse. Anyway, we hung around together, had fun, drank wine, ate food the boys brought over, smoked grass, and went back and forth between the apartments.

A spaced out guy showed up from who knows where one night and ensconced himself in my kitchen to recite his poetry. I thought I might never get rid of him, but when he lost his audience he split.

After Dee went home and the boys went back to Texas, things quieted down quite a lot. That's when I decided I was ready to take my first acid trip.

I went over to sit in the kitchen with Sunny early one evening, took a deep breath, downed the tab with water, and sat back to wait for the trip to begin.

I waited…and then waited some more.

A bit of a disappointment, I was thinking, but just as I was about to give up, I got the taste – a distinctive, almost tactile sensation letting me know I was coming on, getting high.

The music started to sound really powerful. It was Ravi Shankar on the sitar. Groovy.

The petals of the chrysanthemum on the table started moving, growing, opening. It was lovely, and I thought – well, if the perception of time thing in my brain was messed up, I might really be seeing them move. Like in a stop action movie.

That made me smile.

I was getting pretty mellow, until my father called. Pam had picked up the phone over at my place and gave him the number here. She thought she had to, and I thought I had to talk to him since he'd called. Acid logic, I guess.

Anyway, he hadn't heard from me in a while and wanted to check in.

We chatted a few minutes. Lord knows what I said, but then it was over. Sunny told me later that it seemed to be a rule that someone always called or showed up on your first trip. I wish she'd told me that earlier. It kind of threw me a little, and I probably didn't make much sense to him on the phone.

It didn't bum me out or anything. I just wished he'd called at another time.

That was all.

My first trip and it wasn't much more than a super-grass stoned. I wondered what all the fuss was about.

I finally got to meet Sunny's "great man" when Jason showed up at the apartment and asked her to come back to work for him.

This was the "great man"? I mean, I just couldn't see it. He was tall, dark, good looking in a boyish way, sort of like Tony Perkins before *Psycho,* but nothing special. Oh, well. No accounting for taste.

Sunny went back to work at his office in the building next to the Straight Theater. She was also, I was sure, trying to get back together with him. I didn't know how much of her progress on that front was just her wishful thinking, but I didn't say anything.

When his office needed painting, I bought the paint and went with her to help get the job done. Jason reimbursed me with three of Owsley's White Lightning tabs. Acid from the master chemist himself. Wow, very cool, and I wondered if it would be different than my first trip.

CHAPTER SIX

Oh, brother! Was it ever different..

I don't know why I picked a gray day, but then there wasn't much choice that spring.

The fog was in, the sky was a muddy white, and the wind was bitter. The first acid trip hadn't been such a big deal, so I felt comfortable dropping alone.

I sat in my apartment, put a couple of pillows on top of the foam slab and unfinished door I used for a couch, put on a Beatles record, and took one of the White Lightening tabs. While I waited to come on, I threw the coins for the *I Ching* and read what it said. I don't remember much about it, just something about "difficulty at the beginning."

The acid came on fast. No waiting around this time. The funny taste was suddenly there and my body felt as if it were floating.

I was a little frightened, but it felt incredible! Like a roller coaster and I tried to go with it. I looked across the room at my painting on the wall and the white and blue broke into planes of color and line that flowed and vibrated. The sounds from my stereo were soft and strangely muted.

So many pretty visuals, everywhere I looked, and then (so soon?) the record finished and the machine switched off with a click.

The room filled with a palpable, dark silence. All I could hear was the whirr of the refrigerator and an occasional car passing on the street below.

I was alone. So alone – like I'd always been.

If I could only turn the record over, hear some music, but the record player was far, far away, in the distance, across the room under that strange painting, and the floor kept shifting between us.

Oh, my God! I remembered that there was a lit cigarette in an ash tray someplace. In all the shifting visions, I couldn't find it.

Fire! I'd burn to death!

Where was the floor? Everything was moving, like water. Nothing seemed solid.

Was the floor even there? If I put my foot down, would I fall forever? Or drown?

Fall and not be able to move?

I was alone and so scared. I could trust nothing, certainly not my senses, and not even the fact that I could not trust myself.

I don't know how, but I found the phone in my hand – maybe it had been there all along. I wanted to call Zander, and all the numbers melted and flowed into each other. By closing one eye, I managed after a while to call him for help.

When I hung up, I wondered if I had really called him or only imagined it.

Did time pass? It must have: the doorbell rang. I don't know how, but I managed to get up and through the beaded curtain, which danced around me and I had to close my eyes to make my way through the waterfall of sparkling color to ring the front door buzzer.

I stumbled back and settled in my warm place on the padded bench against the wall, hugging my knees. Diffraction patterns were all over the place, on the edges and corners of things, in every nick in a surface. Everything shimmered.

Pretty. If only I wasn't so scared...

Oh, no, no. When Zander came in, I thought I'd made a mistake in calling him. He looked and sounded diabolical with his Hungarian accent and his goatee.

No, I couldn't trust him either. He tried to talk to me, and I distrusted his words.

He held out his hand to give me a stone he'd painted and covered with runes. I laughed.

The stone wasn't it, wasn't what I had been thinking and needing.

Still, I did appreciate the gesture.

He put some music on and lay on the floor as we listened. When he saw that I had settled down a bit, he asked me when I took the acid.

Oh! Oh, yes! I took acid!

I'd forgotten that. Now I remembered. Yes, I'd come down eventually; this wasn't forever.

Okay then. I could breathe; it was all cool.

Everything shifted again and I saw Zander looking a little like a Chinese sage, not in costume or place, but in aura. Whatever that was.

I still didn't trust him, really, but I told myself I had to trust someone. Zander had been good enough to trust when I was straight, so I had to trust him when I was stoned. He was all I had.

I decided to practice pragmatic trust: if it turned out he was not trustworthy, then I'd be able to trust that information. It would be a start.

Thoughts came and went. One would occur and I'd start to tell Zander about it and my mind would pursue and examine it and analogous things on down a line of reason, and I would suddenly realize I'd started to say…something, and it was now so long gone on a train of thought there was no way to end my sentence, so I laughed.

I understood a lot of slang now, like "freaked out," "spaced out," and "turned on." I understood the hippie bells and beads and all the strobe lights and diffraction patterns and the swirls of color. I understood the strange sounds of current music and the seemingly nonsensical collections of words.

So that's what they meant by "psychedelic." Words couldn't describe it; they were too feeble, but every once in a while, they could be suggestive.

We went up on the roof for a bit, and I watched the clouds and admired The City. Then I donned my derby and we went to the deli. I found the world strange, and I was a little paranoid. People looked sometimes beautiful and sometimes eerie and dangerous.

Zander got something to eat, but I couldn't eat anything. I wasn't hungry at all and by then I was starting to come down, so Zander took me home to get a little rest.

I tried to take a nap and sleep eluded me. I was coming down, yes, but I still had some of the visuals and the hyper zing-zing of thoughts.

It was late afternoon by then, and I decided to go across the hall and see Sunny. I wanted to tell her about my trip and see how she was. She'd been really upset and depressed the night before.

Their apartment was silent and no one answered my knock. The door wasn't locked, as usual, and I walked in. Everything was dark and quiet. All the lights were out, yet the dying sunlight still came through the windows. I glanced through the open bathroom door in passing on my way to the kitchen. Sunny's clothes were on the floor by the tub, which was all in shadows.

Something was very wrong, and my heart was tight as I walked into the bathroom and glanced into the tub: I saw a body covered in blood and I ran out of the bathroom screaming, "Oh, no! NO!"

A voice from the bathroom, hers, asked what the matter was.

I nearly collapsed and gasped, "Oh, Jesus, I thought …"

I went out on the back porch to sit in what was left of the sunshine, to breathe and quiet my racing heart. She got dressed and came out to join me. I told her what I had seen and what I had been through that morning.

"No wonder you were so freaked out. You're probably still stoned. Let me see your eyes – oh, yeah, all pupil," she laughed.

"Here," she said, handing me a joint, "have a toke; it'll help take the edge off."

It really did. Just inhaling, I felt my muscles relax, my heart calm.

"Good thing your Zander was around," she said. Stopping for a moment, she smiled broadly, and asked, "So… what's the story between you two?"

I rolled my eyes. "We're just old friends."

"Doesn't sound like that to me."

"Well, it's true. We are very old and very good friends. That's it, I promise. I've thought about it once or twice, sure," I shrugged. "But, it's never happened, and I think that's just as well."

She gave me a speculative look and then took my hand in hers, and very quietly asked, "You're still a virgin, aren't you."

I blushed and got flip, "Yeah. Don't let the word get out.

It would ruin my image."

"What about girls?"

I froze.

"It's okay," she said. "I knew when I first met you. And, I know sometimes you get a little uptight about me and how close we are in a lot of ways."

I retrieved my hand and managed to resist the impulse to bolt. "I've never slept with anyone," I said, "not anyone."

"But something's happened, hasn't it? I can tell."

I looked down.

She waited a moment and then asked me if I would tell her about it.

I'd never told anyone, not really. It was no big deal, except that for me, it was.

Zander was there, but he didn't see everything.

CHAPTER SEVEN

Okay, my "difficult" friends were gay.

Gwen, I'd known since my sophomore year back east. She'd been raised abroad, mostly in Europe, and I found her exotic because she'd travelled so widely and spoke several languages. She was very sophisticated and quite pretty with her blond hair and a model's sculptured good looks.

I don't know what she saw in me, but she sort of picked up with me during a summer session and the next year we were always together. There were rumors about us; people liked to talk and we ignored them. After all, she was engaged and leaving at the end of the year to get married. She was obviously straight, and I was, well, whatever they thought, I was nothing and nothing was happening between us. Nothing.

Frankly, I couldn't bear the idea. From everything I'd read, homosexuals were pathological and sick. There were names for such people, clinical names, uncomplimentary epithets, and obscenities. I'd been called some before, and I'd even used a few on other people, declaring my difference from them.

Mostly, I made a point of not feeling anything romantic for anyone. At least, I tried not to.

I did get pretty depressed after Gwen got married and transferred to her husband's school. I was suddenly alone again and classes didn't have much appeal. That's when I dropped out and kicked around in Evanston and Chicago.

We wrote long letters for a while, but it wasn't the same. I really missed her, and then she stopped writing. After several months of silence, she wrote me out of the blue that her marriage was over and she was now with a woman.

I was pretty shocked and then devastated. I couldn't say anything – to her, to anybody around me, and certainly not to myself, although my dreams were not so cooperative. Dee was a lifesaver: a cross country road trip, leaving everything behind and no forwarding address was just what I needed. I could leave Gwen and everything behind; I could start over.

I didn't forget her, unfortunately, but we did lose track of each other for a long time.

Then – and I was learning that you can trust things like that to happen in San Francisco – I ran into her and her girlfriend, Liz, one afternoon when Zander and I were walking down the beach towards Sutro's to go skating.

I was speechless, but Gwen seemed happy to see me.

She hadn't changed a bit, and it turned out she'd been in The City a year longer than I had, both of them going to grad school at SF State. I suppose it was surprising we hadn't seen each other on campus, but I was mostly there at night and they were there during the day. Now, here we were, chatting away on the beach. Damn.

Liz kept to the background and watched what was going on with amusement, I thought, but maybe it was only nervousness. She was tall and slender, rather attractive, I thought, with her auburn hair and pale skin. She and I didn't talk; we didn't have much of anything to say to each other at that point.

Anyway, Gwen ended up inviting us to dinner at their place in the Sunset after we finished at the rink. Somehow, she made it difficult to turn down the invitation, so we went. It was an okay evening and I got hooked in again. The original friendship resumed in an episodic fashion and without Zander most of the time. He was always polite, but he wasn't all that crazy about either of them.

I never understood Gwen. Never.

We were like those characters in the French movie that came out about that time, *Jules and Jim*. I didn't understand the relationships in the film either (and neither did the characters), but I certainly recognized them. Painful, confusing, compelling passions.

Sometimes, I'd sit around at their place and we'd drink together. Gwen didn't drink much, but Liz could really put it away. She became my mentor for heavy drinking and helped toughen my skin with her insults. Liz smiled when she delivered them, taking the sting out, if not the intent. She had no idea why Gwen liked me, thought I wasn't very bright, and let me know she thought I was hung up and neurotic.

On the other hand, she confided in me, was often the one issuing invitations, and several times put her arm around my shoulders as if we were buddies as we walked someplace. Gwen would sit back and watch. She had thoughts about it, but I couldn't tell what they were.

It all came to a head a year and a half ago. Zander and I were both over at their place for a drunken weekend. I think Gwen and Liz had been fighting…there was that kind of tension in the air and a bit of sniping between the two of them. I got the feeling it might be worse if Zander and I weren't there and, although we both started to get a bit uncomfortable and wanted to go, they didn't want us to leave and we ended up staying.

What happened?

Nothing much as far as anyone else was concerned, I'm sure. That probably made it all the worse for me.

We'd been drinking all afternoon and hadn't bothered to turn on the lights as the sun went down. I don't know how it got started, but we began playing a stupid game of "pass it on" where one person would do something to the person next to them, whisper something, touch them, whatever, and they would say or do the same thing to the person on the other side and so forth around a circle. Then it got to be kissing, and I objected. Liz teased me and called me a wet blanket. I didn't care.

Then Gwen grabbed me by the hand and pulled me up to "help her get more drinks." Down the hallway she dragged me, into the dark kitchen, and then she turned, wrapped her body around me, and kissed me.

I think my nervous system short-circuited.

People didn't often touch me, even in passing. When they did, I'd freeze or jump in surprise. When I rode the bus, people avoided sitting next to me until the seats were all taken and the aisles were crowded. Really. That was the kind of vibe I gave off.

Now, there was this person, a warm, live human being making full body contact. I think I was too surprised to stiffen, but my shock must have shown; when she let me go and stepped away, she laughed. Then she patted me on the cheek and said, "I've wanted to do that for a long time."

At which point, she grabbed a bottle of wine from the refrigerator and left me there.

What the hell!

I couldn't think. Maybe that was the point, but thinking was all I knew.

The only thing I could liken it to was the time I slugged

down my first shot of straight bourbon. My whole body had flushed with warmth; it washed over and through me. Intoxicating, literally.

This…the warmth and softness, the urgency of closeness, the energy of desire…No! I didn't want…but also, yes. God damn it!

When I woke up early the next morning on their couch, Zander was gone. Gwen and Liz were still asleep in their bedroom, and I had a hell of a hangover as well as an unhappy acceptance that people had been right about me all along: I was a fucking homosexual.

Worse, I was in love with Gwen and always had been.

Oh, shit! Wonderful. I was hopeless and screwed up, and, of course, she was impossible and I was stuck.

Oh, God! What a mess!

What to do? I couldn't think of anything, so I wrote them a letter. I told them all that stuff and said I was backing off, going away, and I wished them well. I left the letter on their coffee table and split before they got up.

It could have all been very civilized, we could all have gone on our own twisted ways, but no…no, they wouldn't let me go. It was nuts. Why did I go over there again? Because they told me to? Lord knows, but I did.

Gwen dismissed the whole thing as meaningless, while Liz teased and sent barbs my way. I don't know why, but I let her. I should have stopped her, but I didn't, and…maybe I felt guilty, I don't know.

I let it go on for a long time. Months and months. Until another drunken night, at my place for a change, when Liz started to needle and insult Dee, who was up from LA again.

It was one thing for Liz to get on my case: I always thought I deserved it in some way, but nobody messed with my friends. Nobody.

I took Liz by the arm and threw her out. I pushed her through the front door and down the steps. There she turned and looked up at me in surprise. "You're throwing me out?"

"Yes," I said and then held the door open for Gwen to join her.

Zander cheered when I told him the story. He'd always thought they were a nasty piece of work.

That was our last meeting.

Well…at least I thought it might be.

Gwen had a habit of turning up in my life. The meeting on the beach wasn't the first or last. I couldn't be sure if this was the end of our on again/off again friendship (or whatever it was) or only the beginning of another time-out.

Maybe the uncertainty helped keep the feelings fresh for me.

Anyway, after the kiss, I did decide one thing: if I wasn't doing anything, then I wasn't anything. I was asexual.

That label, I could handle.

I gave Sunny an abbreviated version of the story, leaving out that it was my first kiss. That would have been just too embarrassing.

She listened quietly, nodding from time to time. When I finished, she told me I was getting too hung up on what I thought rather than simply 'being' the beautiful woman I was. Besides, she thought I was wrong in my conclusions and, if I got out of my own way, I'd come to realize that.

Blew my mind, she did, and – I don't know how, but I felt that she'd released me from my self-hatred and fears. For the moment, at least, I felt I could relax a little.

I learned a lot that second trip, but it was heavy stuff

and hard for me. It was like being born again. Terror and an explosion of light followed by pain and fear. Then, I had learned to trust someone, even if it was only because I had no other choice.

I had learned about my fears, and I survived. I didn't think I could ever again be as frightened as I was that day. There was power in that.

CHAPTER EIGHT

The next morning, Sunny wanted to go over to the Haight to talk to Jason about some matter or another and asked me to tag along. She seemed a bit edgy, wanted my company, but not to talk about whatever was bothering her. Okay; I was game.

She brushed her long blond hair until it gleamed, slipped into her best bell-bottoms, put on a long sleeved blouse, donned her prettiest beads, and strapped on some sandals. (Bare feet in the parks were one thing, city streets another.) Time to hit the road.

She expected to hitch a ride, but I could spare some change, so we took the bus instead, got off near the Straight Theater, and walked down to Jason's office. At this end of the Haight, the streets weren't so crowded and they were also quieter. Sunny told me things would liven up in a couple of hours.

I waited outside and could see them through a window, standing in the doorway to his office in deep conversation. She was standing close in front of him, looking up at him and saying something rather impassioned from the way her hands moved. He had his arms crossed and didn't seem receptive. Finally, he uncrossed his arms and turned away while she was in mid-sentence, walked into his office, and closed the door firmly behind him.

She stood there a moment, as if she might try to follow him, and then thought better of it.

"C'mon…let's get out of here," she said making no

attempt to wipe away her tears. She let them fall and went on about her business.

I admired that…being upset yet not done in by it.

She never said, but I was pretty sure he'd rejected her once again.

It was only three days later that Sandra came to get me at the diner: Jason had beaten up Sunny and she was…well, not okay. Sandra thought I should come home as soon as I could.

When I got there, the apartment was dark and Sunny was lying on the bed in the corner mumbling.

Jesus, she looked like hell! Hair all over the place, face streaked, and Sandra said Sunny had a big lump on the back of her head. I tried to get a look at it, but Sunny fought me off and complained that the light hurt her eyes.

I wanted to fix things, but that wasn't possible. All I could do was try to find out what had happened to her. Since she wasn't talking, I called Jason for the information.

Before I could get two words out, he started to run a trip on me about their fight, trying to explain or justify, I guess, but I told him I didn't care. I only wanted to know about the head injury. He finally pulled himself together enough to ask me how she was acting and then told me he'd come over.

I wasn't so sure about the wisdom of that, but if she needed to see a doctor, he was the only one of us with a car.

When he finished looking at her, he came into the kitchen and sat down with me.

"I think she's alright; I've seen her like this before."

"Great," I said. "That's fine for you, we haven't, and it scares the shit out of us. Jesus, man, everyone tells me what a gentle soul you are, and you do this? What were you thinking? What's wrong with you?"

He tried explaining himself again, making excuses, and I wasn't buying any of it. There were simply no good reasons. I managed to keep quiet, and we took her over to the Park Station Emergency Room. The doctor said she had a slight concussion and would be okay, just to keep her quiet.

Fat chance of that. The very next day, the landlord called their apartment to tell them he was going to kick them all out for not paying the rent. Pam told me about it, and I phoned him back to explain that one of the girls had been in an accident. He was very upset and made the right sounds, sure, but I could tell he was worried more about his rent, so I said I would pay it.

Paying their rent on top of buying groceries…I was effectively supporting them. It was okay up to a point. I liked being helpful, yeah, but lately I'd started getting a bit uncomfortable about it all.

I was very close to Sunny, and I liked her a lot. Maybe too much? I wasn't sure.

I was taking on more and more for all of them, and it just didn't feel right. For the moment, I'd wait and hope that patience and time would clear things up. Anyway, I went down to LA to visit Dee for a few days. I'd promised to bring her some acid and sit with her for her first trip. Travelling gave me a chance to get a little distance and perspective for myself.

Dee thought I was being used. I said it was fine, and that I knew what I was doing (even if I didn't).

When I got back, Sunny was back to her old self and

really happy to see me. She gave me a big hug and promptly launched into a bunch of stories and plans she was eager to tell me.

"I need to start making connections," she said. "I need to find a way to pay the rent and so forth. You, Sandra, and Pam have done enough for me. Besides, I think they're getting ready to split (they're never around these days), and I know you're getting a little uptight with it all, too.

"I'm going to hitch down to Topanga next week to see a couple of people I know. Brent Dangerfield is going to be there with his old lady. He's a producer and sound man for a few bands and an old friend. I'm sure he can turn me on to some gigs."

CHAPTER NINE

I hadn't seen Zander in some weeks. What with the closing of Sutro's and all (that was a real bummer), we hadn't been skating in a while. We weren't all that crazy about the rink downtown (it had no character or history), but now it was the only game in town, so we capitulated. It was time for us to do a bit of catching up.

He picked me up on his old motorcycle, and I prayed it would hold together. He'd managed to get the Triumph running again, but it was always a bit of a crap shoot.

The downtown rink wasn't as big or as nice as the old Sutro's, but the figure skaters were as annoying as ever. Such superior attitudes. It was fine that they got the center of the rink to practice their moves, but when they started spinning, bending their bodies over and holding their legs out straight, those shiny blades were just about face height. And, sometimes, they'd drift toward the outside and our lane. It made me a bit nervous, and I tried to stay close to the rail as I circled the rink.

Zander and I had our own kangaroo skin speed skates with their long thin blades. We'd bought them after watching the speed skaters out at Sutro's. Man, were they fast! And there was a wonderful grace and ease about them when they got up to speed and were bent forward, swinging their right arms, holding their left behind their backs to keep their balance. Very cool.

So we got speed skates. It wasn't like we wanted to race

or anything; we just wanted to skate the way those guys did, and you couldn't do it on figure or hockey skates. Besides, I had to admit that what I really loved was shaving ice with those long blades as I came in for a stop. I mean – Shooosh. Yeah, like that…sending up a lovely spray of ice. Always made me smile.

Besides, I found it vaguely therapeutic to go around in circles on purpose for a change. The faster the better.

Taking a break, we got some coffee and sat down at a little table to talk.

He didn't want to say anything about his girlfriend for a change, and I suspected the relationship was going south, so I didn't press him. He'd talk when he was ready, so I caught him up to date with what was happening with me and the girls across the hall.

He stopped me when I mentioned dropping acid again.

"Really? Even after that bad trip? Are you sure that's smart?"

"Well," I said, "it ended up being 'hard' rather than bad. I learned a lot."

He raised an eyebrow, so I tried to explain. "It's like I was behind a dirty window under cotton batting and couldn't see what was really out there or feel much of anything. When I was on acid, the barriers were down, the glass cleared."

"Hmm." He leaned back in his chair, took a sip of coffee, and asked, "Did you see God?"

"No, you jerk," and I took a mock swipe at him, which he easily ducked. (It was part of our usual routine.)

Then…and I should have seen it coming…he got that look: eyes wide open, all innocent seeming, but not making real contact, looking up and a little to the side with a sly glance. And then, there it was: a bomb, a perfectly terrible pun.

When I groaned, his shoulders started to shake, and he laughed that full-bodied laugh of his. He was sooo fucking pleased with himself.

I could never remember what any of the puns were afterwards. I think that was self-defense, to forget them, to refuse to make a place in my memory banks for those noxious pests. If he was any indication, they might breed there.

I pictured big nameless puns rattling around in his head surrounded by scurrying little ones begging for attention.

On a more serious note, I tried to get Zander to go with me to the big march against the war, the "mobilization" they called it. I thought he'd be all for protesting considering his brush with the military, but he couldn't get away.

Later, I found that the girls at home had other things to do, so I ended up going by myself.

People must have started congregating early in the morning, because by the time I got there, the various organizers had their areas set up and big banners to show people where to line up. I found myself a place to the side where I could fall in behind the main group when they started moving.

Meanwhile, it was contained confusion. Some marchers brought their own homemade signs or picked up placards with slogans from somewhere, and the organizers lined people up, making sure the folks with banners led off. Other people walked and ran around, talked with friends, carried messages. Lots of excitement.

At some magical moment, a whistle blew and everyone started moving forward. The mob coalesced into a stream and then a river that ran relatively smoothly up the street. Additional marchers (like me) fell into the current from the crowd at various points, while news people stood on street corners with microphones, and cameramen ran back and forth in front of the march taking pictures.

Some people sang songs, others shouted slogans. On the sidelines, some people cheered, while others heckled the marchers and yelled epithets. One or two threw things or engaged with a marcher until they were dragged off by the cops.

The march ended at Kezar Stadium where some podiums had been set up. Organizers and assorted celebrities gave speeches through bull horns, calling for action of various sorts, getting roars of approval from the crowd.

When I was marching along, in the thick of things or along the sidelines, it was kind of exciting. All that energy and comradery...I felt part of something really big.

Then, when the speeches started, the feeling fizzled out leaving me feeling a bit empty and hung over. I was against the war and all, but political rhetoric and rabble-rousing left me cold. It reminded me of gospel meetings, and true believers kind of spooked me, so I figured it was time to go home.

※

Sunny got back from LA after just a couple of days.

It hadn't gone well. She said the scene had changed since last year, and she hadn't been able to accomplish much. Saw some friends and all, but didn't get a paying job.

So…now what? Rent was going to be due again, all too soon, for both of us, and I couldn't afford to keep both apartments going. There was only one logical path, so I asked if it would be cool if I moved in with them.

What could they say? Of course it was fine, and now, at least, there was only one rent to pay. We moved my stuff into the apartment, and it was a bit more crowded, but kind of groovy, too. There were always a couple of animals and a lot of people there and more kept coming and going. We had as many as ten people one time and that was too much for my head. I had to escape periodically to the back steps for fresh air and relative quiet.

I started thinking that if I was going to live like this, maybe it was time for me to drop out and quit my job. Frankly, I couldn't hack being the breadwinner, and I was also starting to lose it at work. Ten or twelve months had always been about my max to tolerate counter work.

I threw the coins for the *I Ching* asking what I should do now and didn't get anything I could understand. Thrown back on my own resources, I decided to write a letter to an old friend. I might or might not send it; sometimes just writing a letter was useful for me to figure out where my head was at.

Dear Brit,

No comment on my last letter. Daunted, but still unbowed by silence, I continue.

You're one of the few people from my old college days I'm still in contact with and letter writing is usually such a drag these days that I do little of it. What I can express in words seems to meet with shock, fear, disapproval, or fascinated desire to know more than I can or wish to convey. So, I don't write (except to you), I move around, and, without trying to, I have effectively disappeared. My friends here know where I am and that's about it.

I've quit my job, but it's not really a drop out move, even if it turns out to be. I'd always figured I'd stick it out until I got bored and/or couldn't stand it anymore. The time came when dealing with the public was a bitch, and I decided to quit before I turned into one.

I really like work, hard physical work; it leaves my mind free for other things. The job had that, but it also had the public. They were groovy more often than not, but a drain on me emotionally.

I don't know what I'm going to do now, but I don't have to decide anything today. The sun is shining; there's a big pot of food on the stove and plenty of cigarettes, wine, beer, grass, and music.

I've moved in with my neighbors…for the moment. We have to get out next month. There are four of us in a three room apartment plus a German shepherd, a poodle, and a neighbor's cat (a big gray tom) who hangs out here. Plus, there are always people who show up to crash on our floor.

Dig the situation:

> Terry: yours truly, 26, Aries, worker, "the intellectual" (their label for me)

> Sunny: 24, Aquarius, emotional center, artist

> Sandra: 20, Leo, working for no pay at the Straight Theater, enthusiasm

Pam: 19, Taurus, silent, stony

Wolf: Sandra's German shepherd

Cuddles: Pam's poodle

(The cat is just "The Cat")

Good surface interaction and cooperation, amazingly so. Well, maybe not. The balance of roles and personalities is good, yes; underneath, however, are the personal, internal hassles.

I have a few anxieties about my role; Sunny has hers. The younger ones are still having family problems, especially Sandra. You know…attraction to and rejection of the status-quo, the whole family routine.

My announcement that I'd dropped out and quit my job was greeted with silence. Not TOTAL silence, just silence about the subject. It meant that I had rejected my role, and they're now busy figuring out their own trips. No decisions had to be made as long as I was paying the bills. Waiting was possible and extended.

I'm learning a great deal, and although I am convinced of nothing else, I believe I am becoming a better person. Happier anyway, which makes me a lot easier to get along with.

I figure you're wondering, so yes, I am taking acid. Four trips so far and it's been hard work for me. The trippy visuals are groovy, but minor and simply the easiest to talk about – maybe that's why it's usually the only thing you hear.

I seem to be reliving my life. I was about age six the last time. I go back with my adult perceptions and look around the world as I perceived it. True catharsis seems possible, and I'm not afraid.

No, wait: I am afraid. I'm afraid of the vision of myself pursuing life as I was. The stimulus of LSD is something I can't fight intellectually. I can't resist. I am forced to see and deal with what I see, to grow.

What I saw around me now was real, simple, and basic: no one was working and no one was talking about, let alone in a position to pay the bills and rent.

All right then. I could always get a new job when my money ran out, maybe one that would utilize my degree, but when I mentioned that option to Sunny, she wasn't happy with me.

"You do that and I will take off. I'll never forgive you if you go back to work to support us."

Well, forget that then. I'd try to think of another way.

Sometimes, the gods do provide – about that time, Leah, my old landlady from when I'd been in school, gave me a call.

We were pretty tight now, but when I'd first rented the room off her garage, she had made a point of telling me she wanted it to be strictly business. We shared a bathroom and I had kitchen privileges, but she had her life, I had mine, and we'd go our own ways.

I hadn't expected anything else, so that was fine with me. Then, when I was studying late for an exam one night, she brought down a tray of cookies and milk for me. After that she frequently invited me to her Sunday brunches, and we became friends besides being tenant and landlady. Pretty groovy old gal and we'd stayed in touch after I moved out.

Anyway…she called to see if I was interested in a little job. She knew a couple over in Mill Valley who needed a house and dog sitter for five days while they went out of town. Would I be interested?

I took a quick look around the room at all the mess. Maybe if I wasn't there it would encourage the girls to help themselves a little more. So, I said, "Sure. What's the deal?"

"Well, they'd pick you up next Wednesday and drive you over, show you the place and introduce you to the dog (Goldie's a sweetie). You'd take care of the place, walk the dog, feed her, etc. They'll pay you $25, and you can help yourself to what food's available. What do you think?"

"Sounds perfect to me."

"Oh, no drugs, you understand? And it's just supposed to be you, not your friends."

"Of course. No problem. And, Leah, thanks for getting me the job."

I left Sunny with three bucks, some food in the refrigerator, and a pack of cigarettes and went down to the street with a small bag of my stuff to wait for the Bentley's.

They were on time, and I got to introduce myself to Goldie, their golden retriever, who was sitting at the back of their station wagon. The couple seemed nice, the dog was really cool, and their house back in the hills was nice looking and had a good size yard and great views.

I got a ten minute tour and they were off.

I stowed my gear in the guest room and wandered around with Goldie at my heels.

A note on the fridge said that everything in the pantry and in the fridge (but not the freezer) was fair game. I opened the door and there was a treasure trove of food. Wow! I hadn't seen a refrigerator like that in a long time and there was a lot of food to choose from. I would not be going hungry.

The den had a big TV and stereo, and there was quite a collection of classical, jazz, and folk music. Not much rock, but that was okay; I could do with a break. I hadn't watched TV in a really long time, so I grabbed a coke from the refrigerator and some potato chips from the pantry and sat down on the couch with Goldie to watch some dumb TV. (The soaps were a hoot.)

I ate and snacked when I felt like it. All the quiet was a great relief and I slept a lot. I also got days of alone time I must have really needed, and Goldie was a love. We went for long walks and then cuddled up on the couch or played ball. Dogs are such simple, uncomplicated beasts.

It took me a while to get antsy and by then, the Bentley's were back.

Goldie jumped all over them, Mrs. B. went off (to take a quick survey of the house, I figured), and Mr. B. unloaded their stuff and stowed my bag in the wagon. I gave him a report, such as it was. It had all been pretty uneventful, once I'd figured out how to work the appliances, and I'd stripped the bed and washed the sheets and towels.

When Mrs. B. got back, she was all smiles and handed me an envelope with my payment. Everything was cool.

I said good-bye to Goldie, and we were off to The City.

Walking into the apartment was surreal and not in a good way. Man, what a contrast to Mill Valley!

For one thing, the place was dark and smelled bad. The air was loaded with a miasma of odors – rotting stew on the stove; stale dirt on the floors; overflowing, fetid garbage cans; sickly people sweat; dusty, ungroomed animals; and the sharp tang of old urine on the floor by the toilet. Enough to make my eyes water.

Sunny was on her bed facing the wall, and when she turned over she looked terrible. She told me the story of her latest freak out, and I tried to help her, but it was difficult getting through to her. I asked her where the girls were and she didn't know. They'd gone off some place.

So, it was up to me. I sighed and started to clean the place up; no one was going to feel better the way it was, that was for sure.

Life pretended to go back to what passed for normal, but this time I knew it wasn't all "peace and love." Underneath all the light and music, there was…I didn't know what to call it, but it wasn't good. I told myself that while it might be fine to throw myself on the mercy of the universe, at some point I might just have to get up and see about saving myself.

For right now, the money I'd made house sitting was almost gone already. I needed to think about food and getting some money again. I made the rounds of my friends who fed me and laid a couple of dollars on me as I was leaving. That held us for a few days more.

Sandra finally reappeared one night, bringing home a guy and a bag of groceries. Billy was a long-haired, cute looking musician (drummer) who was heading back to New York.

He was a real talker, and he went on and on, which annoyed me and amused Sunny. She was feeling better and the fact that Billy was obviously impressed with her didn't hurt her opinion of him. Kind of pissed off Sandra, though.

Sunny took me aside and put me down for not paying attention to him. "He's a man, after all," she whispered to me. "We, as women, have to listen."

Really? Later I told her that if I bought into her man trip in its totality, I would have to jump off the bridge. She just patted my hand, said she knew I felt that way, and thought as time went on, I might come to see things differently.

I had my doubts.

Sunny had her ups and downs, and without the gigs working for Jason anymore, they were more often downs. Mostly these days, she couldn't paint or write and would just sit looking lousy and pain ridden, plagued by self-doubt.

I reminded her that, "God looks after mad men and innocents."

It was something I often said of and to Sunny, adding that she was both, which always made her laugh. I'd say it hopefully, reassuringly, and sometimes with a touch of cynicism.

Pam wandered in one day, grabbed a few things and then went off again with scarcely a word. Sunny and I looked at each other and then shrugged. The kids were obviously getting ready to fly the coop, just maybe not quite yet.

Sunny sort of woke up after that and flashed on the fact we had only $1.76 among us and very little food. She mustered up her courage and determination, dressed up, and went out on a hunt for big game. She walked into the Playboy Club's Public Relations office to pitch herself, her watercolors, and her writings.

I was stunned when she came back elated. She'd blown their minds and then they blew hers by asking her to bring in more of her work next week. No money now, but if it worked out they said that she could be looking at big things, like film, TV, and magazine articles. This was a testing period, they said, an assignment to see if she had discipline and creativity under pressure.

She said they were excited and hopeful of good results.

Very, very groovy. Frankly, I'd been wondering if she wasn't inflating things.

I was going through changes about Sunny these days, and not for the first time. I had doubts about her, about me, and twinges of jealousy and protectiveness. My latest repressed homosexual tendencies hanging me up, no doubt. I hoped that they were merely minor attacks of backsliding, but sometimes I'd look in the mirror and hear my old record play, saying 'What are you doing? Who do you think you are? Oh, yeah – maybe you're getting better, but damned slowly. I really wonder if you're worth the trouble.

Even when I wasn't looking in the mirror, I could sometimes hear that voice.

CHAPTER TEN

Sandra split for New York with Billy and Wolf, while Pam still wandered in and out of the apartment doing nothing. Not exactly good company, and when Sunny decided to look for a temporary gig in the Haight, I went along.

She knew a lot of people and walking up Haight was a stop-and-go matter as she ducked into stores to talk to old friends and hailed others on the street. We might share a joint with them, and some were, I gathered, local celebrities, even if I didn't recognize the names. Bobby Snofox, a guy named Resner, and Luther Greene, to name a few. She told me about a talk she'd gone to with Alan Watts and about partying with a band, the Jefferson Airplane.

She pointed out the Diggers' Free Store where they gave away food and clothing and anything else they could find. Seems they didn't believe in private property and thought everything belonged to everybody. I wondered how that worked, but before I could ask, Sunny dragged me off to the park where they'd set up a free food table.

Before we got all the way there, however, we ran into David. Sunny had met him some time back in the winter through mutual friends. He was in with a number of the Haight merchants, a couple of the bands, and the local dope dealers. He gave her a big hug and a terrific smile and invited us over for a meal, so we turned back and went along with him.

David didn't look much like a hippie. If anything, he

looked like a college boy, maybe an engineering student with his white shirt and khakis. No beard or mustache, and his dark brown hair wasn't all that long by Haight standards, more like one of the Beatles in the early days. He had this very young, very open look about him, really warm and welcoming, not uptight at all.

His commune was one part of a triplex up on Masonic. On the door at the right was a piece of paper with a quote from the Tao Te Ching:

In the pursuit of learning,
every day something is acquired.
In the pursuit of Tao,
every day something is dropped.
Less and less is done
Until non-action is achieved.
When nothing is done, nothing is left undone.

David saw me reading and laughed, explaining that it was from his morning reading. "It reminded me of how little I really know."

He led us up a long flight of steps to the second level and a seven-room flat. Sandalwood incense drifted down the hallway, and I could hear music from one of the two rooms in the back of the flat. My mouth watered at the smell of spaghetti sauce which must have been coming from the kitchen.

From the front rooms, I heard sounds of laughter and voices through an open door to one of the front rooms, and someone was on the payphone in the hall.

We grabbed plates of food in the kitchen and joined the group up front sitting around talking. Old Jim (to dif-

ferentiate him from "Young Jim" in one of the back rooms)
sat cross-legged on a mattress on the floor, leaning against
a wall covered with madras bedspreads, and rolling a joint.

He was one of the last of the Beatniks and had migrated
to the Haight from North Beach when he was priced out
of his digs there and needed to find lower rent. He actually
looked more like a calendar picture of an old hippie with his
long gray hair and beard, sunglasses even in doors, tons of
beads and bracelets, torn jeans, a brightly patterned woven
sash of some sort he used for a belt, and Mexican sandals.

He finished rolling the joint and passed it around saying
goodbye to people. He was out on bail from a marijuana
bust for possession in Santa Cruz and was going to trial
soon. David tried to reassure him that because of his age
(forty-eight) and how little pot they found on him, they'd
put him on probation or something. Old Jim didn't seem
so sure. In any case, even if it turned out well for him, he
didn't think he'd come back. He wanted a warmer place,
maybe San Diego, and, after this wet spring, a dryer place,
too. David told him he'd hold a room for him until he got
word of how it went in court.

Carl, a skinny guy with a big mass of light brown hair
and a thin moustache, a line beneath his nose that he kept
fingering, sat next to him and seemed more than a little
sorry to see him go. Seems Old Jim had been good friends
with Carl's parents when he was growing up, a sort of uncle
to him.

Carl's folks had headed south last year, and he wasn't
exactly sure where they were. I somehow gathered that they
didn't tell him their plans, and for some reason I wondered
if they'd dumped him. Or maybe just forgot about him.
Kind of sad.

I found a piece of floor where I could put a cushion and lean against the wall, and I settled in to listen to the music from KMPX and the conversations. The house dog, Tex (some sort of spunky terrier mix), came in and found himself a place where he could survey the room and keep an eye on things. He was such a self-possessed little creature and his erect ears that flopped over at the top made him look especially alert and smart. I had to smile. Damned if he hadn't made himself a calm and collected space in the midst of a bunch of stoned hippies.

Pretty cool, and I found it interesting that although he sat near David, he wasn't his dog. A guy passing through had left him there. David and Tex were friends and all, but Tex was still waiting to meet his person. At least that's what David said, and Tex didn't object.

I was pretty sure he understood what was being said, but maybe that was the grass.

Another joint made the rounds on a jeweled alligator clip, and we ate and talked a while. It felt really easy and comfortable there. Nice place, nice people, and they all seemed basically happy and content, even Old Jim.

Days passed, a week, then two, and nothing materialized, at least no money, from the Playboy talks, and it was time to move.

Pam and her poodle had been staying with "friends" someplace "nearby" – it was all pretty vague, and then, suddenly, she was gone. Only Sunny and I were left, and David said we could move into his place.

Cool, but while everyone there knew Sunny, they didn't know me. I had to sit down with the residents for a little intro and pow-wow to see if I wanted to move in and if they thought that would be okay.

David gave me a little briefing first. "Now that Old Jim's gone for a while, you're going to be the oldest person around. Not by many years, but some people may like it and others not. Also, you're the only one who's got a college degree, but several of us have a bit of school under our belts and some are just naturally smart. You understand what I'm saying?"

"Yeah, I get it. There's no problem; I don't think I'm special on either count."

"Good. One more thing: please don't ask about families, where people grew up, brothers and sisters, that normal sort of thing. Actually, don't ask about their pasts at all. There are a lot of people in the Haight who don't want to talk about the past for very good reasons. If they want you to know, they'll volunteer the information."

We all sat down in the music room at the back of the house.

Young Jim, a tall lanky guy with lots of dark hair stood by the door, like he was ready to bolt at any moment. At least that's the way I thought he felt. I might have wanted to split, too, if Elizabeth were sitting in front of me. She was his "old lady" and quite an intimidating presence, even when not standing. A big woman, with light brown wavy hair, piercing gray eyes, and what appeared to be a permanent frown.

Next to her on the floor, was Sally, a little blond bit of a thing. The word that sprang to mind was "wispy." She looked very young and as if the wind could pick her up and carry her off.

Across the room sat Carl who stopped playing with

the stereo long enough to sit down with us and roll a joint.

I said hello and told them I'd only recently dropped out, had never lived in a commune, but looked forward to it. I said I was more than willing to do my share and knew that I could benefit from their experience.

Elizabeth asked me if I ate meat and she said the word with such disgust, I figured she was a vegetarian. I admitted that I did, but not all the time. She told me that she, young Jim, and Sally were following macrobiotic diets (a purer, healthier, more positive regimen, I gathered) and would not be eating with us when we had meat. They would cook their own meals and use their own dishes and utensils.

Sally had other concerns. "What do you do for fun? How are you on concerts and dancing in the park, that sort of thing?" she asked, rather hopefully, I thought.

"I'm afraid I don't much like big crowds. I get to feeling claustrophobic, you know. Still, I might go down to stand around the edges sometimes.

"Mostly, I read a lot," I concluded, shrugging apologetically.

She looked positively deflated. "Oh. Another thinker, like David. I was hoping for someone to play with."

They asked me a few more questions, and then I asked a few about house responsibilities, what they would expect of me, and so forth.

They told me they shared things and took care of each other, but there weren't any written rules or anything.

Elizabeth gave me a final look and summed up her thoughts. "Well, I would have preferred a vegetarian, but at least you're another woman. We need to balance out the men in this house. The yin and yang have been all out of whack for a long time. So, it's fine with me if you move in."

Young Jim just nodded, and the others said yes. Carl had to say that another woman was always fine with him as he passed me the joint.

I was in. All I had to do now was pay David my rent and move.

I went through my books and, hard as it was, I managed to reduce my shelf space. I took a bunch of boxes of the rejects out to the college book store and downtown to a dealer to see what I could get for them. Not a bad haul and I had the first month's rent plus a few bucks.

Sunny told me David was letting her stay at the commune without paying for now. That was pretty cool of him, I thought, and when I said so, she agreed and looked off into the distance for a minute before she added that she thought he was an old soul and very spiritual without being all macho or anything.

Something about the way she said it…well, if that was the way it was going to go, all I could hope was that David didn't turn out to be like Jason.

Fortunately for us, David said he had a friend, Earl, who owned a van and the two of them would help us move. A big help – I'd moved before on street cars and on foot, making lots of trips with heavy boxes, and it wasn't fun.

We met up at the commune on moving day, and I knew who Earl was right away. He didn't look like an engineering student like David, more like a philosophy major or something else in the humanities. He was tall and thin, wore glasses, had curly hair, and was clean shaven. No chinos for him: he wore nice slacks, a crew neck sweater, and a college jacket.

He seemed to cultivate a vague, sort of goofy/stupid look, but David told me later he actually had a PhD in astrophysics. He'd had been a prof at Stanford for a while, until he dropped out. I didn't think he looked old enough for that and learned he was only twenty-one. Really? So he must be a genius; that was cool.

Anyway, the guys changed into jeans and work clothes and got ready to get sweaty. David put on a faded red sweat shirt and Earl wore a torn blue work shirt over a white T-shirt which had seen better days.

Besides the usual boxes of household stuff, I had more boxes of books – heavy boxes, and David laughed when I explained that I had some favorite friends in them.

"Lots of friends, huh?"

I smiled, but it was true, I did love my books. I could get rid of some, but I always managed to carry a number around with me when I moved. They were like memories; I might not take them down to read again, but I was always happy to see them there on the shelf.

Anyway, Sunny stayed in the van arranging the boxes, furniture, and kitchen things while we went up and down the steps clearing things out. I took care of finding a safe place for the typewriter myself (it was even more of a friend than my books).

Near the end, Sunny left for an appointment of some sort.

After I took a look around upstairs to see what remained, I told Cat we were splitting, closed the windows on him, and took over arranging some things in the van for the last load. That's where I was when I heard yelling from inside the building.

When I got through the front door, I saw the guys and the refrigerator perilously balanced at the top of the steps coming down from the apartment. They were staring wide-eyed at my landlord, who was screaming at them from below about stealing his property and saying he was going to call the cops.

I yelled out to the guys, "The refrigerator's not mine; take it back," and immediately smiled at my red-faced landlord and apologized, saying I'd neglected to tell them it wasn't mine, and I was so sorry. Luckily, that seemed to mollify him.

They got the refrigerator back in the apartment without doing any damage to themselves or the walls and mumbled apologies to my landlord as they came down. We all got in the truck and, after the doors shut, we looked at each other and fell apart with laughter.

"We were so close!" said Earl. "Another five minutes and we would have had it."

"I don't know," I said. "It looked pretty iffy up there. I thought for sure you were all going to come crashing down at any minute."

"Oh, well," said David. "There'll be other opportunities."

BOOK TWO

The Summer of Love

(May to August, 1967)

CHAPTER ELEVEN

The commune members played musical rooms after Old Jim split.
When everyone finally settled down, I was in the little room
across from the kitchen, David and his dog in one of the
big front rooms and Sunny in the other. Carl was still in
what had been a dining room in the old days, between the
kitchen and front room, and Sally was in one of the back
rooms, while Young Jim and Elizabeth shared the other.

With a place for me to live taken care of, I started getting
occasional temp work downtown and bought food when-
ever I could. Without a refrigerator, I had to buy things that
would last (onions, potatoes, canned goods) or that would
be eaten up at the next meal.

Most of the time Sunny and I shared the cooking for
everyone. Well, not the macrobiotic people – Jim, Elizabeth,
and Sally. They didn't even want to be in the same room
with any of our food, and not just when we had meat, which
was rare enough. At meal times, they retired to their rooms
to eat brown rice and some thin soup that seemed to be a
staple of their diet.

Surprised the hell out of me to learn they were meth
heads and most of them were shooting up – Sally being
the exception (she took pills). All of Elizabeth's stuff about
preserving the purity of their food and bodies and they were
shooting speed? I never understood the logic of that. But
then it took me a while to figure out a lot of things.

I had assumed all was groovy in the commune and that

this would be simply a larger version of what we'd had on 18th Street.

Technically, it was a commune, sure, but communal living is hard. Getting everyone to contribute equally on one level or another, depending on how much money or what skills they had, was one thing, and then balancing personalities another. Here, unfortunately, the sharing didn't seem to be equal again. David footed the bill for most of the rent and utilities. Jim had money from his family, Carl had a part-time gig, and other people contributed what they could, but, as near as I could figure, that was often nothing.

Right off the bat, there were clashes between Sunny and Elizabeth. Two matriarch types or maybe earth mothers, was bad enough, but I didn't think an Aquarius like Sunny and a Virgo like Elizabeth would ever get along really well. No, not when Sunny had so many fire things going on in her chart and, I suspected, Elizabeth had a lot of water stuff in hers.

I tried to keep the peace, and at the same time not get hung up in any of their conflicts. When I was in doubt about what to do or say, I looked around for things I could fix, as usual.

The door on Jim and Elizabeth's room had been driving them crazy, hanging off the hinge because the screw holes had been stripped out. I filled in the holes with glue and a couple of broken up toothpicks. I let that dry overnight and the next day, rehung the door. Nicely done, if I say so myself. Elizabeth laid a little string of beads on me as a thank you.

I don't think Sunny thought much of my doing Elizabeth favors, but shortly afterwards, fortunately or unfortunately, Elizabeth came down with hepatitis and took to her bed. Jim came down with it next, and right on his heels, Sally. I took a guess that she'd been playing around with shooting up. She moved in with Elizabeth and Jim and they all took to their beds for the duration.

Tough stuff, but Sally and Jim seemed to get over it okay after a couple of weeks. Elizabeth wasn't so lucky and had a bad case. At least she lost her energy for confrontations and we had peace in the house.

David and Sunny started to be a pair. It was probably inevitable that the two Aquarians would find each other, but it did create a few tensions. Sally, it turned out, had a crush on David, and Carl had some fantasy about having a thing with Sunny, so neither of them was very happy.

I was actually okay with it all. It wasn't that much of a surprise to me, for one thing, and for another, I really liked David and had a lot of respect for him. I think it also relieved me of any of my feelings of responsibility for Sunny. Besides, we were still close…sisters and all, so I was fine.

More than anything, it was kind of reassuring. Maybe it wasn't a homosexual thing between me and Sunny, after all. Maybe it was more of a sister thing. I'd never had a sister, so I kind of liked the idea. Of course she was the wiser sister, even if she was younger. I didn't mind that; what I did envy a bit was their…what shall I call it? "couple-hood"? I wished I had something like that.

Anyway, Sunny moved into David's front room, and David kept the other front room open for Old Jim until he found out what was going to happen to him. Besides, it made for a good place for the occasional crashers coming through the front door, as well as drug deal negotiations.

There was another nonpaying resident: the house ghost. I guess like a house dog, every house had to have some sort of spirit. Ours was an old lady, a previous tenant, people figured, who appeared from time to time down the hall, back by the kitchen, giving off cold and disapproving vibes. Both Jim and Carl swore that they'd seen her when they were tripping. Carl called her "the gray lady" and said she was really uptight.

I never saw her myself, but I will confess that I found it a little creepy at night by the back rooms. Sometimes, there would be a cold draft and, try as we might, we could never track down the source of it.

At one of the house meetings, we decided we should try being nice and respectful to her. We started to say things like, "Excuse me, ma'am" and "Good evening" and stuff like that when we were down there at night. Why not? Seemed little enough to do and the boys didn't see her as frequently after that, so maybe…As for me, I called her "Mrs. Gray" and she didn't seem to object. I still didn't see her, but every once in a while I would just get a weird feeling.

What really stirred her up was some of our visitors. It couldn't have been a coincidence that things mysteriously broke or spilled when some strangers were around.

※

Outside in the Haight, things were calming down a bit. People who had arrived at the first part of the year had settled in, and the hordes expected in the summer had not yet arrived, so there was lots of time for people to talk about stuff. And talk and talk…

Sunny grabbed me by the arm one evening and pulled me back out of the door I'd just come in.

"C'mon. There's an Elder Gathering over on the Pan-handle. You need to hear these men. Really wise souls."

I was beat and not in the mood, but I didn't seem

to have any choice.

We got there a bit late and were relegated to peeking around a hallway corner at the speakers in the living room. I didn't know who any of those guys were. Maybe I was supposed to, but they only looked to me like four balding and bearded middle-aged guys at the front of a room filled with cigarette and grass smoke.

Every bit of the floor was taken up by someone sitting at their feet. Sunny made her way through the crowd, trying for a better position. I was happy to stay where I was.

Whoever they were, they all seemed to have followers, people who hung on their every word. Gurus of some sort, I guessed. Certainly the tone was there – deep sonorous rumbles, serious wisdom, and they went on and on. Lots of name dropping, and I made out Ginsberg, Leery, Watts, and Snyder among them.

I wondered how the hell I managed to get roped into this. I was tired and bored already. I wanted to leave, but there were too many people behind me now. I checked to see where Sunny was and she'd found a place even closer to all her "great men" and sat there smiling. Wonderful, I thought; I was never going to get out of there.

It had only been about thirty interminable minutes when a man came in, the person whose place it was, I figured, and he said we had to break things up. The cops had got a call about a "pot party." A few people wanted to protest and were talked out of it. The owner promised that they could reconvene the next night.

I was saved, and Sunny was all charged up by what she'd heard and relayed it to me on the way home. Lots of Buddhist this and that and Age of Aquarius stuff. She finally caught on that I wasn't saying anything and asked me what was going on.

"It's just not my thing: a bunch of old men sitting around pontificating and telling me what I should believe. Always irritates me."

"I thought you liked philosophical discussions."

"I like the questions; I don't usually like the answers people come up with."

"Maybe you should try listening with an open mind every once in a while."

Ouch. I apologized and said I was really tired and all. She seemed to accept that. Enough anyway. I knew I was intolerant about some things, some people. I didn't like it in myself, but I guess, like a lot of intolerant people, it didn't bother me enough to change. Okay, maybe I even got off on it a bit. Damn; I really was no different than a lot of people I didn't like.

So, no, maybe it wasn't the same between Sunny and me as it had been on 18th Street. We were still close, but there we'd related mostly with each other and had each other's back. Sometimes, I'd felt she gave me more than I gave her, but how could you quantify things like that? Anyway, now that we were in the Haight, things had changed. Of course, she had David, and there were more people to relate to (one way or another), lots more acid, the ongoing pressures of survival, the drama about what was happening in and to the Haight, and…well, it was all different. Still, even if she wasn't as available for me as she had been, I was sure she'd step up if I needed her.

I missed what we'd had, but I was okay. I was kind of busy learning to see myself more clearly, who I was, what I wanted, and what I would and would not do to survive. I was stronger than I'd thought, maybe even braver. (The jury was out on that one.) For sure I was learning how to live in a group situation with lots of different people.

Differences…yes, but there were funny little things that were the same. Like, on Masonic and in other houses, the floorplans were pretty similar and the sounds were the always the same. The music for one thing, of course, but there also seemed to be a sort of pattern or rhythm to our lives. Everywhere, I heard a chorus of doors opening and closing, bare feet and boots racing up steps and down hallways, bells ringing, people laughing. And, the smell of sandalwood soap and oriental incense, pot, sometimes hash, floated down every hallway and out their doors.

If I walked into the wrong house, I might not realize it for a while.

Mostly, I dropped acid in the front rooms and stayed with Sunny and David or in my own room, but there was a great setup in Sally's room at the back. We called it the "music room" and there was quite a collection of equipment and albums. I went back there to trip one time for a change, but as I started to come on, really feel the acid working, the music kind of freaked me out. Maybe it was the album playing, one of the Rolling Stones' and they can be pretty heavy handed. Anyway, lots of heavy bass and droning repetitions bummed me out a bit. I moved back to the front room after a few minutes of that and was cool again. Much better vibe up there, for me, anyway, and a lot of sunshine came through the front windows.

Although … those windows really needed cleaning. When I was tripping, I always noticed things like that: dirt and clutter. Drove me crazy, but I couldn't do anything about it until the next day. Then I turned into a cleaning maniac.

In our house, as in other communes, the women took care of most of the cleaning and cooking, looking after their houses and their "old men." The men made noises about looking after their "old ladies," dealt some dope, had part-time jobs, sometimes even full-time gigs. Others panhandled, ran errands for the rock bands, worked at the Fillmore or the Straight Theatre, had family money, or were on welfare or Social Security disability. A few of the guys, I regret to say, simply sat around and let the women do everything.

David paid the bills and he also chipped in on the cleaning, taking responsibility for scrubbing the bathroom and taking out the garbage, thank God. I was really impressed by that; usually when a bunch of guys lived together, they were beasts and any woman around was stuck with putting the seat down and generally cleaning up after them. David seemed a lot older than his years and really responsible.

The macrobiotic folks took care of their own kitchen things and their space, while Sunny and I handled most of the rest. Since Carl had a part-time job, he seemed to feel exempt.

Carl was kind of a funny guy, at least when he wasn't sulking. Guys like that don't often have a sense of humor, but if you gave him a joint when he was grumpy, he mellowed right out and saw humor in some weird things. A little twisted, I thought.

Like, one night, late, when Elizabeth, Sally, Sunny, and I were in the kitchen, he came pounding up the stairs, grinning from ear to ear, excited and eager to tell us a story.

"You guys should have been there. Man! It was far fucking out."

He sat down with us at the kitchen table, took a deep toke as a joint passed, and began.

"You know Bobby's old lady? Sarah? She's been huge for months and we were talking last week, wondering when she'd finally have the kid. Well, she did it tonight!

"I was over at Bobby's to score some weed and hang out a while. He's got some great tapes of music you can't hear anywhere else and great weed; we got really wasted. Sarah hasn't been smoking any since she got PG, so she just left us to it and went off to start cooking.

"I guess she was gone a while but, you know how it is, it could have been five minutes or an hour, and then she was suddenly back, shaking Bobby.

'The baby's coming!' she yells. 'We've got to go!'

"All Bobby could say was, 'Wow, man. That is so groovy!'

"So, she pulled him up and poked at him to get going, but he couldn't do anything except move real slow. He looked kinda confused, mumbled something about her not getting so upset and being more serene. She looked ready to hit him, and I was sitting back watching, grooving on all this primal stuff, you know?"

About this time David, Jim, and a couple of guys they did business with came into see what all was happening. Carl filled them in and then went on.

"Anyway, when Sarah noticed me, she asked if I could drive shift.

"I said I could and she threw the keys at me before I could tell her I didn't have a license. She said, 'Get the car! Bobby can't drive shift even when he's straight and he sure can't now. It's up to you.' Then she started moaning and grabbed a chair to hold onto.

"Pretty heavy, huh? Anyway, I tried to get a little straight and ran down the hall yelling for help from the others in the house, but some people turned away and others went back to offer Sarah suggestions like, 'Lie down,' and 'You should get up and walk,' that sort of thing. Not real helpful.

"Sarah kept batting them away, but when Beth arrived, she grabbed her hand hard and wouldn't let go. So Beth took over and started giving orders. (She's a tough one, Beth.)

"Anyway, she told me to get the car and when I told her I didn't have a driver's license, she said, 'So what? You can drive, can't you?'

"Yeah," I said, "but…"

"'But nothing: get the car. Now! Go!'"

"Don't know quite how I did it, but eventually I got the car out front with the motor running. They bundled Sarah down the steps and onto the back seat, and Beth climbed in with her. Bobby and me were up front and he passed me a joint as I pulled away. Cool, huh?

"I offered Beth a hit, but she only said, 'Drive, damn it!' Real harsh, so I passed it back to Bobby and tried to keep the car in its lane and not go too fast."

The guys were all laughing at this point in Carl's story, getting a kick out of the idea of him driving at 5 miles an hour and Bobby being so out of it.

Sunny, Elizabeth, and I just looked at each other. I knew we were wondering how Sarah was doing during all that. Probably scared, hurting, and furious.

It took him forever, probably as long as it took for him to get to the hospital, to get to the part in the story where Sarah actually delivered the baby – in the hospital and not the car, thank God.

"It didn't seem to take long," he said, "before the nurse came out to say she'd had a seven pound baby boy. Wow! Bobby was pretty psyched. He told me they were going to name him, 'Bear' – that's his totem animal.

"Pretty groovy story, huh?"

It was time for Sunny to bring him down to earth. "So... how are Sarah and little Bear doing?"

"Huh?" Carl seemed surprised at the question. "Uh, okay, I guess."

"You 'guess'?"

"Well, yeah. We left her at the hospital and came home."

"You and Bobby?"

Now he seemed confused and looked to the others for support. Catching Sunny's tone, they carefully looked at anything but him.

Finally Sunny said, "Never mind," and we left them there to make our own plans for visiting Sarah and getting her some things for when the baby came home.

Maybe Carl wasn't as funny as he thought.

CHAPTER TWELVE

Spring, a season for babies and the rain, which continued to fall at record rates.

People made jokes about Noah and wondered if they should start building ships and gathering the animals. Lots of people got sick, too, and when they were sick they stayed sick for long periods of time.

The first month or so in the Haight, I had a few dollars from before and then a few more from time to time with temp jobs. The refrigerator (David and Earl finally scored a free one from a dope customer up in Bernal Heights) and pantry always seemed a bit bare, but a lot of people seemed to come and go in the house, and we tried to keep at least a pot of rice on the stove. Not ideal, but still food, and when one or the other of us got paid, we ate pretty well for a couple of days.

Cigarettes were the real obsession. In the front part of the house, we all started out smoking different brands but when money got short, that was impossible. Twenty-five cents a pack was simply too much for us to spend. Luckily, Bull Durham rolling tobacco, the stuff that comes in a little cloth bag, only cost eight cents, but the Bull Durham rolling papers weren't gummed, so I had to shell out another few cents for a pack of Zig-Zag gummed papers and borrow Carl's rolling machine, a godsend for those, like me, who had never mastered the art of rolling our own.

When money got even shorter and we couldn't afford

even a bag of Bull Durham, we pulled tobacco from the butts we'd prudently saved and rolled that. Sometimes we even got to the point where we had to roll the butts of butts, sticky with tobacco tar. Pretty desperate fare.

Well, what with the rain and all, I got sick, and my lungs hurt. Maybe that also had something to do with those "butt cigarettes" or both the rain and cigarettes. Having so little food sure didn't help.

I couldn't do any temp work when I was sick, but at least I was over twenty-one and a state resident. I took myself downtown and applied for welfare. I thought I might have pleurisy and a doc looked me over suspiciously. He had lots of questions and, I don't know, maybe he thought I was faking it, but he finally approved me anyway. I got some vouchers to hold me over until my welfare checks started coming in and I gave one to David for rent and took the other to the grocery store.

Forty dollars a month for rent, and fifty for everything else: food, transportation, toiletries, laundry, etc. Not exactly a fortune, especially when I figured I was buying food for the five to ten people who might be staying at the house. Still, compared to what we'd had (or didn't have), nothing to sneeze at.

I took almost all of the food money down to Littleman's and the Safeway to stock up, while Carl and a few others went out to score toilet paper at the gas station and ketchup and other kinds of food packets from the diners and restaurants. We ate really well for a week, not bad for the second week, scraped by the third, and by the fourth we kept checking the pantry to see if something had magically appeared.

※

Carl brought home a bunch of magazines that were being thrown out at the shop where he worked, and it was a trip reading what the outside world had to say about us. I mean the TV and the press could not seem to get over what was happening in San Francisco. Every day there was something new being said about us or rehashed.

The word was out that something very exciting and special was happening. We already knew that, but now everyone did. Then, a lot of the big rock bands came out with songs about it and a few high profile personalities made the Haight sound like a kind of Coney Island Shangri-La.

It was all over when the Mamas and the Papas came out with the "San Francisco" song. It promised all sorts of wonderful things to anyone who would come here. More people started looking our way and the big shots said that fifty to as many as a hundred thousand people would arrive in the Haight by June.

That many? Holy cow! Really?

Yes, really.

This wasn't a big enough neighborhood to handle that population. Besides, almost all of the new people would be young and have no money or any place to stay. What would they do? How was The City…or, for that matter, how were we going to cope with such a crowd?

The Diggers had been cool, handing out food and finding people places to crash, but there simply wasn't enough floor space anywhere for all those new people. The Diggers didn't have enough food or beds, and even if they found more, what would we do with the mobs and the inevitable trash and bad trips?

Out on the highways, we heard that lots of long haired boys and girls were hitchhiking west. Old VW vans, ancient cars, and beat up trucks chugged along the roads, breaking down or just running out of gas. Rumor had it that the farmers, used to helping their neighbors and maybe remembering their parents' stories about the Dust Bowl, fed them, helped them fix their cars, topped up the gas tanks, and even slipped them a few bucks. At least at first.

When interviewed, they said the young people reminded them (in some ways) of their own kids. They looked a little funny with their long hair, but kids were like that, and they talked a little funny, too, but they were Easterners, so…At least they smiled and knew enough to be polite and say thank you.

❋

Tired and elated, the new arrivals reached the end of the line where the rainbow had led them as they made their way over the last hills to the place where it was all happening; where all the lines converged, to the nexus of energy and change, the Age of Aquarius, magic and music: the corner of Haight and Ashbury.

We saw them out there every day that spring and summer, smiling, their arms outstretched, their heads back, looking at the sky, and turning round and round to take it all in.

That only lasted so long and then a questioning look would come into their eyes. Now what? What do we do now? They would shyly buttonhole a stranger on the street, "Hey, man. I'm new in town. Is there someplace I can crash tonight?"

There was always a couch or a bit of floor and, if not,

there was always the park at the end of the street, Golden Gate Park, with acres of trees and bushes under which a sleeping bag could be unrolled. It wasn't so bad, making an aromatic mattress from the big brown eucalyptus leaves.

If they still had a few dollars, they scored dope from one of the salesmen on the street who were dealing from doorways, hawking their wares in competition with the guy in the next doorway. Pot, acid, speed, mescaline, mushrooms, you name it. No hard drugs, like cocaine or heroin – they were too expensive, and their illegalness too well enforced to be handled that openly. But, if that was what you wanted, a dealer would always know someone who knew someone.

Most of the dealers were strictly small time, selling a few joints, a couple of baggies of grass, or a few pills to pay for their own drugs and make a few dollars for food and a place to sleep. At a dollar or two up to maybe five or sometimes even ten for various commodities and quantities, none of us made a lot of money, just enough to get by.

I mostly worked with Brer Rabbit. He was a sweet guy and drove around on a motorcycle with a tame rabbit who stayed in a crate on the back when he was making deals. He always had great acid and would front me for some tabs or whatever. I'd sell them and then pay him back. He'd give me a free hit or a little baggie of grass for my trouble.

Not exactly big dope deals.

It was only May and already people seemed to be sleeping anywhere they could on the streets and in the park and whatever shelters went up. They panhandled, sold dope and souvenirs to tourists, and Lord knows what else. A few of the merchants on the Haight would give them fifty cents for sweeping in front of their stores, stuff like that, but none of it went very far. You could get some fish and chips down near the park or maybe some pierogis at the Russian diner but not much more. One meal, maybe the only one of the day, and still no place to sleep.

David brought home people he found wandering the streets sometimes to crash with us. One guy stayed with us for a week, hardly speaking a word, and then tried to OD on aspirin. He made himself good and sick, and I talked him into going to the emergency room. He didn't want to go, said he didn't have any money, but I told him they'd help him get on Social Security and the disabled program, if only so they'd get paid.

Kind of a bummer, that whole scene, so when Sunny scored a handful of concert tickets from her old friend, Jason, I decided to give it a shot. We all needed a change of atmosphere, so Sunny, Sally, Carl, and I clutched our little silver and red tickets and went over to the Fillmore to listen to Big Brother and the Steve Miller Blues Band. Great music, and it wasn't long before everybody was dancing up a storm, jumping all over the place, flailing their arms…sort of free-style, I supposed. It wasn't for me: I'd never learned how to dance.

When I was growing up all the boys went to dance classes to learn the fox trot and waltzes and stuff. Dances with real steps and a system for learning them, I guess. I didn't know where other girls learned, but my mother seemed to think I'd learn how to dance from them. She couldn't see that I didn't have any girlfriends to teach me.

Now, Sunny was telling me that all I had to do was get out there and "move to the music." Oh, sure. I'd seen the people out there bumping into and falling all over the ones who moved gracefully and in rhythm with the music. I knew which one of those I'd be. No thanks.

They all went out on the floor and did their thing, while I hid out and listened to the music, watched people, and beat a hasty retreat through a nearby exit door when I got too overwhelmed by the strobe lights, sound level, smoke of various kinds, and, of course, all the people.

To think the Fillmore "only" held a thousand or two people; over at the Winterland they could handle five times that. It was enough to make me bolt through the door just thinking about it.

A couple of weeks later our attempted suicide showed back up at the front door, bringing rice and canned goods as a thank you gift. He was on disability now and had a place in a group home to bed down. Nice how all that worked out for him.

Other people showed up on our doorstep from time to time, sometimes with David or other times with a scribbled address in their hand they'd been given for a crash pad. We did our best to accommodate them for at least a night and then they split, going home, to another house, to Canada to avoid the draft, or sometimes just disappearing.

CHAPTER THIRTEEN

Food was getting scarce again and we were down to the last pound of rice in the bag. I was sitting around the kitchen table with Sunny and Sally (she was taking a break from the macrobiotic gang to hang with us for a change). David was doing a dope deal in the front room with two college kids from Stanford. He had a couple of keys of grass for them, and that would go a long way to getting the June rent money and a little more food on the table.

We were handing around a joint and sipping on glasses of lovely, orange apricot nectar from a big pitcher, and talking about who knows what, when Sally looked up to ask if any of us knew what the Tao quotation David had posted over the table meant.

Look, it cannot be seen – it is beyond form.
Listen, it cannot be heard – it is beyond sound.
Grasp, it cannot be held. It is intangible.

Sunny and I had to laugh, and we told her not to worry. Even David himself sometimes didn't know what the quotes meant. We all laughed then, shrugged, and were filling our glasses with more of the apricot nectar when Sally started laughing and nearly fell off her chair. Well, that got us laughing too, and it was a while before we could get her to say what was so funny. She was sputtering, but finally choked out, "Apricot nectar! We don't have money for that! It's only orange Kool-Aid!"

Really? I could have sworn…but that's all it was. We'd fooled ourselves.

Well, it was pretty hysterical and we all went off in a round of laughter, vastly amused at ourselves until Carl came in and glared at us from the doorway.

"You're laughing, and I'm hungry."

"There's a little left over rice from lunch," said Sally.

"I'm sick of plain rice, I want some real food."

"We're all hungry," said Sunny, letting a little exasperation with him creep into her voice.

I didn't know what he expected from us and said so.

"Well, some of the girls in other houses go out and turn tricks for their old men. Like Charlie's girls!" he said, looking pointedly at Sally.

She cringed and became impossibly small, so I stood up protectively and stared him down.

We were all just looking at him now, very quietly and obviously not happy with him.

"Well, they do!" he protested.

"Well, we're not," I said. "Go away."

He went, mumbling all the way up the hall and slammed his door. We looked at each other and shook our heads.

"Can you believe him? What a nerve," I said.

"I don't know what's wrong with him these days," said Sunny.

"What was that he said about 'Charlie' – who's he?" I asked.

"Oh, just a guy over on Cole with a group of people he calls his 'family' or something," said Sunny. "They're from LA, and you know how they can be. He's set himself up to be a kind of big deal, but I know a guy, Gary – he was living at Bobby's place last winter? Anyway, Gary started hanging around with Charlie and his group. He thought Charlie had a lot to say, but then he got the vibe Charlie was getting involved in black magic or something really bad. Lots of negative energy and scary stuff. Gary got spooked and split."

"Well, Carl had better not get too impressed by him," I said, and we were a little quiet with our own thoughts for a few minutes.

Finally, Sally broke the mood with a giggle.

We looked over at her, restored to her normal size, and saw her grin.

"Penny candy?" she proposed.

"Yes!" we chorused.

One of the Stanford boys had taken a break to pee and we took advantage of the time to hit up David and the other college boy for two quarters.

The three of us ran down to Haight Street and to the candy shop, laughing and talking about our favorites, working ourselves into a sugar frenzy.

We tumbled into the long and narrow store with its counter on the left and hundreds of jars and display bins of so many different kinds of candy that we were stopped dead in our tracks, dazzled by the color, the variety, and the sweet smell in the air.

The owner was an old guy, maybe forty or more, but he smiled at us like he knew what we'd been up to (and he probably did).

Each bin had a little hand-written sign indicating "2 for a Penny," "Penny Candy," etc. all the way up to "Five Cents" for big bars of various kinds of candy and chocolate bars.

In our price range, there were long, waxed paper strips with pastel sugar drops that came in six inch lengths, little yellow twists of Bit-O-Honey, Mary Janes (a peanut butter toffee – my all-time favorite), little wax bottles filled with a sweet syrup, Necco wafers, tiny root beer barrels, small boxes of candy cigarettes, paper wrapped tootsie rolls, peppermint sticks, and…and…God! So many choices!

We agonized over our decisions, and the guy behind the counter was sweet enough to throw in an extra penny candy so we could each have seventeen. We took ten each for ourselves and then brought the rest back to the house to share.

Not exactly equal shares, but when it came to candy when you had the munchies, well, there were limitations.

That night I heard a scream from the back of the house, a really horrible sound, and I jumped up to see what was going on. Had someone broken in? Was anyone hurt?

I found Elizabeth on the floor by Sally's bed trying to hold Sally who was flailing around only half awake, screaming, and crying. I sat down with them, added a friendly arm, and made what I hoped were soothing sounds.

Sally finally stopped screaming after a while; her trembling took a bit longer to go away. We got her back into bed, and I grabbed a blanket to cover her. Exhausted, eventually she drifted off, and Elizabeth tucked her in.

"Quite a nightmare," I said, as Elizabeth softly closed the door behind us.

"Yeah, she gets them every now and then. Something will trigger them and she won't say what they're about. I don't push; I've got an idea about them."

I gave her a questioning look, but she shook her head and went back to her room.

✳

The next day, Carl had the good sense to apologize. He said someone had laid a little smack on him. He was only snorting, not shooting up, but that's what smack did to him.

Elizabeth gave him the evil eye, and Sally looked down at her feet. I ignored him, and eventually he went away.

I'd never been interested in opiates, and Carl certainly didn't make it tempting. Aside from the meth at the back of the house, we mostly used only acid and grass. Oh, every once in a while someone would show up with some mescaline, mushrooms, Ritalin, or hash, but usually we stuck with the basics.

(I tried hash a couple of times and got really, really depressed. Definitely not my drug of choice.)

Lately, word had started going around about a new drug cooked up by an Owsley apprentice called STP. It was supposed to be a heavy duty psychedelic that would keep you stoned for days. Some people were intrigued, like Sunny, but I didn't want to be stoned all that long. I told her I liked short trips, not ocean voyages.

David said he'd wait until he learned more about it, and Sunny went along with that.

Good thing, too; that drug was bad news. Sixty percent bad trips, it turned out, and no way down.

CHAPTER FOURTEEN

There was a free concert in the park, over near Hippie Hill, and the sun decided to come out for the occasion. We were still getting a lot of rain that year and thought the sun was some sort of good omen. It seemed like everyone in the Haight was going to the park to enjoy the music and sunshine.

Usually, I only took acid at the house, but Sunny dragged me out to the park for another kind of experience. We both dropped when we got there, along with a group of Sunny's old friends and maybe another hundred or so people. Lots of stoned people out there that day.

The cops stood around the fringes, and a few mounted police walked up and down, but there weren't any problems. Joints were passed, pills sold, and none of the cops seemed to blink at the dealing. Everyone was cool.

When I started to feel the acid come on, I was up at the top of the hill, under the tall trees. I felt sheltered there, but Sunny and her people drifted downwards, so I tried to follow. The crowds and all the people flowed around me in a pattern I could almost, but not quite, figure out. Everyone seemed to be smiling, so I smiled back. I tried to go with the flow and to stay with my people, but inevitably I lost them in one of the various streams.

But, that was okay. I knew where I was and where home was. I figured I'd find a quiet place to be for a while, maybe a place where I could sit and watch everything, the bands and all the people. When I came down, I'd walk home.

One of the bands was playing, and I carefully stepped over the extension cords that reached from a building across the street to the amps in the park. Some Hells Angels guarded the stage and the amps, and I laughed to see a pack of little boys who had appointed themselves to race up and down along the cord and warned people away from the junctions. At their age I would have loved doing that. I almost joined them, but found myself instead over near the old Merry-Go-Round. I had to walk around it, marveling at the animals, the expressions on their faces, and all the bright colors. I thought back to when I was a kid riding one of the horses up and down, around and around, reaching for the brass ring.

They actually had brass rings way back when, not a stupid piece of plastic. But they never let you keep the brass one; they always wanted you to trade it in for some dumb stuffed animal. Oh…yes. I could almost hear the sounds of the carnival now and smell it: the hot sugar of cotton candy swirling, roasting peanuts, and…I suddenly found myself alone by a chain link fence over at the tennis courts, trapped between the fence on my right, a narrow dirt path in front of me, and on my left a dense thicket of rhododendrons with thick, green leaves. I was hemmed in and I could see little but the fence and leaves and…

I remembered being a little girl, tagging along after my big brother, being told he was a boy and could go some-place, do something, but I couldn't go with him, because I was a girl.

I looked at the fence and wondered if it was meant to keep me out or keep me in. Or was it both, depending on the circumstances? I was scared, frustrated, and lost.

Eventually Sunny retrieved me, which was a relief, but I couldn't forget that part of the trip. I recognized the situation, the trap, all too well.

I couldn't talk to Sunny about it. I didn't think she would understand.

Walking back, we passed the tourist bus going the other way. The Grey Line ran "Hippie Tours" through the Haight several times a day. For those of us who enjoyed putting on a show, they could be a great audience, except that some of the tourists stared at us like we were animals in the zoo and didn't smile back when we waved and smiled at them.

It was fun (or funny) at first but it got old fast, and a few of the Diggers took to carrying mirrors down the street holding them up to the busses so the tourists could see themselves. I couldn't remember who it was, but at least one person got on the bus and tried to turn everyone on, much to their horror.

The buses were bad enough, but on the weekends people in cars took their own tours and crowded the streets bumper to bumper. It was hard to simply go about our lives, let alone do a little shopping or dealing on the street in peace.

The icing on the cake, half the people on the street were reporters or sociology/anthropology grad students doing research papers on the "hippie phenomenon."

The "peace and love" hippies were always fabulous to photograph. We had all that long hair, those colorful outfits and costumes. And, of course, there were young girls dancing around with bare midriffs.

We were friendly, mellow, and obliging; we didn't get uptight about much of anything and gladly posed for great photos. Interviewing us, however, could be a problem. It was difficult sometimes to get a complete sentence out of a hippie or one that sounded like it meant something other than mystical rantings.

We were nothing like the others. They would talk your ear off – the Diggers with their manifestos of radical anarchy, the writers at the *Oracle*, even the merchants, and, of course, the Berkeley folks and all the anti-war demonstrators and the civil rights groups, etc. Lots of good quotes and more words than an entire issue of a newspaper.

The reporters and students, for all their protests of neutrality, obviously had many different agendas, and I thought they twisted our words, what we were trying to say. They'd ask about demonstrations by the anti-war and civil rights people as if we were part of that, throwing blood at soldiers, blowing up banks, and sitting in at various places. That wasn't our scene, but they couldn't believe it.

I had to wonder: when they interviewed the kids in Berkeley, did they ask if they carried flowers to put in rifles? I bet that would have got them an earful.

CHAPTER FIFTEEN

Zander had been very busy lately, but now he surfaced to invite me over to his place one Saturday for dinner. He wanted to introduce me to his new girlfriend and would be serving his signature specialty, chicken paprikash. An opportunity to get away from the crowds have a dinner? How could I resist?

It turned out that Carol was an old friend of Zander's next door neighbor, George, up on Potrero Hill. She was another artist, a sculptor/pot maker, and she'd come out from Chicago to stay with her old friend George until she got established. Very quietly, the Hill was becoming quite the artist community. Didn't look it, but a lot of artists lived there, and George was a real craftsman himself, almost a sculptor in wood.

Anyway, George introduced Carol to Zander and, after a while Zander asked her out. I guess that one thing led to another, or was going in that direction. She was a nice looking girl with black hair and blue eyes, always a striking combination.

She reminded me a lot of the artists in my old dorm. The administrators made the mistake of putting them all on one floor in our new dorm. Needless to say and much to their horror, brand new rooms were treated like studios and all the Danish modern décor and furniture were raw materials. I loved visiting them, but was glad I didn't have to try to sleep with all that going on.

Anyway, we ate dinner and chatted away, Carol and I

getting to know each other a little and feeling each other out. I assumed Carol wanted to know if I was competition for Zander, and I wanted to know if she'd feel threatened and want to push me out. The usual.

I asked her about her work, and she offered to show me her stuff when she got her own place and set up a studio. Then, we did a little female solidarity stuff, like I rolled my eyes at something Zander said, she checked out the brother/sister thing we had going, and by the end of the evening, we were on the way to a friendship.

The big surprise of the evening: it came out that she'd never smoked any grass. How had she managed that? I thought a joint came with the title of "artist." Maybe it was because she hadn't lived in the dorms at her school, but, in any case, Zander and I saw to fixing that lack in her education. I'd brought over a couple of joints from David's last deal, a little Jamaican grass, and we passed a joint around after dinner as we talked.

Then, Carol got thirsty and went into the kitchen to get a glass of ice water, while Zander and I sat back and listened to some music. In the background we noted the sound of the refrigerator opening and closing, ice cubes being levered out of the tray, the water turning on then off.

And then the sequence was repeated.

"She's taking a while," I observed.

A few minutes later, he said, "I wonder what the problem is."

Finally, we walked into the kitchen to see what the hell she was up to.

She was staring in befuddlement at three glasses, two ice cube trays, and many ice cubes, some in the glasses, others melting on the counter or in the sink where the water ran freely into the drain.

She looked up and, in plaintive tones, said, "It's so complicated!"

We fell out then, laughing away, and eventually she joined in.

When we recovered, Zander and I both related our own stories about how things could get absurdly out of hand when we were stoned (and he took over getting the water).

"How come it looks so easy when he does it?" she asked watching him. She was feeling a little foolish, and I told her it was only the grass. "It does that. You just need to go with the flow, let yourself be amused, you know. Oh, and wait until you get the munchies!"

She turned to reach up into a cupboard and came out with a nearly empty bag of cookies. "I think I know about that already."

Later in the evening we sat around in the living room and she asked me a lot about what life was like in the Haight and what an LSD trip was all about. The two of them seemed interested in acid, so I said I'd score some for them if they wanted. They decided to think about it; Zander thought Carol ought to get used to grass first, which seemed wise.

It had turned out to be a very nice evening.

It was time for me to drop again. I sat in Sunny and David's room, while he told her about his last trip and the auras he saw. Sunny was sitting with her colored ink pens and tried to draw what he described. Not like a photo or anything. She was trying to capture the feel of them somehow.

I listened to the music they were playing, grooving on the psychedelic song lyrics, and I saw the strange, beautiful, eerie imagery evoked by Procul Harem in "A Whiter Shade of Pale" and the Jefferson Airplane in the "White Rabbit." The lyrics didn't make any sense on the surface, or not much, but sometimes the beauty of it was the message or the humor or even the whimsy and enough. Playing with words and images and sounds. Breaking free from a circumscribed world, expectations, and rules. Discovering that the world didn't fall apart when you dressed, lived, loved, talked, danced, sang, or played at things that were different and far out.

Meaning, there was room in reality for a lot more than I'd been told or believed possible.

The Beats wrote poetry, novels, and other kinds of books.

The hippies didn't write. Their art was visual in posters and auditory in rock music.

Maybe that explained why the rock groups were the era's philosophers and spiritual gurus – most of the hippies didn't read much, but they did listen to music.

Thinking about it, I decided that what acid did for me was break down my barriers and walls. It forced me to see everything at once, things I routinely blocked out without even noticing I was doing it. I wore self-protective blinkers and practiced self-censorship; I needed LSD to really see.

I saw and, having seen, I could no longer be blind.

I had to accept and maybe do something about it, whatever "it" was.

Sometimes, it was pretty banal, like dusty shelves, unwashed dishes, clutter on my desk...things I needed to do to clear my life, help unmuddle my thoughts.

Other times, I saw the cues revealing the state of mind of people around me, what they were hiding, not seeing in themselves and their relationships.

And, when I was troubled, I was forced to see the real reason for it in myself and the sometimes difficult, but necessary, actions I needed to take.

It wasn't always like that. I could also listen to music and find myself transported into the notes and lyrics as if they were a physical playground. I could watch the way light illuminated motes of dust in the sunlight as it shone through a window or how a prism broke the light into separate colors that flowed like water in a river.

I would write about it all, typing on my old Underwood for hours. It helped me remember and to organize my sometimes chaotic thoughts. I used the pages to help me set things up for an acid trip. I could – maybe – control my environment a bit better, provide cues and opportunities for myself in the things I placed around me. But, for all that, the unexpected might still intrude – beautiful things I could not have anticipated, like a rainbow, or, unfortunately, ugliness, like angry voices, tears, dissonance, and I'd be trapped for good or ill, in contemplation of it, helpless to resist or defend myself.

It was then I needed to remember that in order to have a good trip, or at least not a bad one, I needed to be open and accepting. I couldn't fight the experience.

Scary sometimes, oh yes. Bad trips were a reality, as I well knew, but if I could embrace the fear – even if I didn't know that was possible at the time, I might succeed. Maybe not all the time, but at least some of the time. Maybe more than that.

I thought it was worth a try, that "peace and love" were the keys to a lot of things: a good trip, the Haight, the people in my life, and my own, too often tortured self.

Sunny interrupted me about then to laugh and say, "You're thinking too much again."

I think I blushed.

CHAPTER SIXTEEN

Carl asked me to get a big bunch of bananas when I went to the Safeway on my grocery run. I was cool with that: they were on sale and more nutritious than the candy bars he usually asked for (and I refused to buy). I had no idea he was going to grab them all.

"Hey! Wait! Where the hell are you going with those?"

"I just want the skins, not the bananas. I'll bring those back."

"Carl, it doesn't work that way. They'll go bad really fast after they're peeled."

Well, he wanted to argue, and we went round and round until I remembered we had most of the makings for banana bread. So I negotiated to swap the bananas peels for all of the fruit plus fifty cents for walnuts and eggs.

A much better deal for us, and the kitchen smelled heavenly that afternoon as the loaves baked. When I took them out of the oven, I had to beat people off – notably, Carl – in order to let them cool down.

Man, were they good! Moist, sweet, and both smooth and crunchy with nuts. A great treat.

Late the next morning, the aromas Carl cooked up were another story altogether. An acrid, wet burning smell drifted down the hallway from the kitchen, threatening to fill the house.

"What the hell is that?" I complained, coming up the stairs.

David poked his head out of his door to explain, "Carl is cooking banana skins."

"What?"

"Yeah, he heard that's what that song 'Mellow Yellow' is all about. The word is that Donovan was trying to tell us we can get a great high on banana skins. So, Carl is trying to dry out some banana skins he's scraped. Then, he'll pulverize them and smoke the residue."

I must have looked incredulous, because he added, "I know, I know, but Donovan had to be saying something, didn't he?"

He laughed as he went back into his room so I couldn't figure out if he was serious or not.

"At least open the windows, Carl!" I yelled and turned to go out again.

※

After the smell cleared out, after all his smoking only made him cough and failed to produce a high, Carl abandoned banana peels. He had another, less stinky experiment he wanted to try. He took the reel-to-reel tape machine from the Music Room back to his bedroom to play some of the Beatle songs. That would have been fine, but he played them over and over, backward, forward, slower, and faster. Seems he'd heard there were secret messages in the recordings At least that's what the guys down at the music store told him.

Frankly, I couldn't hear a thing, and it was driving all of us a little crazy. So we ganged up on him and made him use headphones and disconnect the speakers. He stayed in his room for hours and hours after that. And, when he reappeared, he had nothing to say about any messages. At least not to us.

Two nights later, we were all sitting around in the front room again, passing a joint, and people were laughing, dropping in and out of conversations, free associating, taking a weird idea and running with it in their own heads, in the words of others, in something heard or seen, a song lyric.

I felt like one puppy in a litter, all of us gathered there, having fun, taking care of each other. It felt really good, warm, and safe.

And, then, of course, Carl had to come in and go on about the tape recorders to this young girl Sally had invited to dinner, and he started coming on to her right away.

"I met a guy who says there are all sorts of messages on the Beatle records," he told her. "Hidden ones. Yeah, really. Maybe you could come to my room a little later to listen to them? You seem like a sensitive person; you could probably hear them clearer than I do." He whispered something else in her ear, and she turned a little red.

He didn't see me roll my eyes or hear me mumbling about what a dog he was. Just as well.

Meanwhile, Glen tripped in a corner, whispering, "Messages. Like Mercury the Messenger god, and do you hear how close 'message' is to 'massage'? Yeah, touch, magical stuff and, oh, wow! Dig it, man: magic and messages and…" He trailed off and closed his eyes.

Glen was a new guy from some little western cow town. Really tall, well over six feet, and he wore plaid flannel shirts, blue jeans, and a big leather belt that looked like it should carry a holster. I said as much about that to him when we first met and he said, "No, ma'am. I never carry a sidearm. My pa said a good Winchester was about all a man ever needed." Then he gave me that little smile of his and said he'd left his rifle at home.

Nice guy really, but it took me a while to get him to stop calling me "ma'am."

David had found him on the street two weeks ago and brought him home, another waif. Naturally, the sound of two sets of footsteps on the stairs had alerted Tex, who gave his single sharp warning "Someone's here!" bark and trotted out to wait for them in the hallway.

He took his job of guarding the house quite seriously, and while he recognized David's brisk steps, he didn't know the new ones that accompanied him. They were slightly heavier and more solid sounding.

At least Glen wasn't the mailman.

Tex really hated that guy.

What is it about mailmen and dogs? Do they feel taunted by his dropping paper objects into their territory? Whatever...Tex would bark insanely at the man and then kill the letters. We tried introducing them to each other, but it quickly became apparent that wasn't going to work. We adapted as well as we could by using a box outside the door.

Anyway, Glen wasn't the mailman and Tex waited patiently to check out the stranger. Seeing Glen, maybe smelling farm smells on him or something, he sat down and cocked his head to the side taking him in.

"That's Tex, the house dog," explained David.

Glen smiled, walked up to him, and stooped to present his hand for an introductory sniff. "Well, howdy there. Imagine a couple of cowboys like us finding ourselves in this here neighborhood."

They did that eyeball to eyeball thing, and then Tex sniffed his hand, looked up at him, wagged his tail, and nosed Glen's hand.

He was inviting a pat; I'd never seen him do that before.

Frankly, I was a little jealous.

Anyway, Glen was pleased to oblige him. "Nice to meet you, too, partner."

Watching them together, I had to wonder if Tex had found his person. Glen certainly had a big grin on his face, and when he stood up to follow David down the hall to the kitchen, Tex fell right in beside him.

Oh, yeah. Well…good for you both. I gave them my blessing.

Glen had only been looking for a place to crash for the night, but when David found out he was a grease monkey and could fix motors, engines, and even clocks, he invited him to stay. Maybe he could get that old washing machine out back to work, and he wouldn't have any trouble getting work fixing the old cars around the Haight.

Glen even had some bread upfront for rent money. We thought he was going to be a real asset. Tex took to sleeping with him the first night, and they made a nice pair – a boy and his dog kind of thing.

That was all fine with David. He had enough on his hands with Sunny. She'd been in a bad head lately and was just pulling out of it.

My mind continued to wander around some more until I suddenly flashed on myself: Wow! That was some good grass! I'd kinda drifted off thinking about Glen and Tex. Now, I was back in the front room and I heard David start to talk about coming to the Haight to Jim, who was sitting next to him and shifted my attention.

Seems like he'd dropped out after his sophomore year at MIT. His dad had wanted him to be an engineer, like he was, and David did okay in school, but he found it all soul-sucking. He'd split last year.

I took advantage of an opening to ask him why he dressed so often in khakis and white shirts, the whole straight uniform thing.

"When I'm dealing, it's better to look like this than hip. Besides, these are the clothes I had, and I didn't want to buy a whole lot of new stuff." He paused and then smiled and added quietly, "It's okay, you know. I have a few other things for concerts and events. I have moments when I'm cool."

David was the only one in the house who was a reader like me. He had books in his room, and he'd go out to the Park Branch Library every couple of days to get more and catch up on what was happening in the newspapers. He kept informed, but he didn't seem to let the news get to him, not too much anyway. He said that he relied on us to tell him if it started making him crazy.

We compared books and his were written by Alan Watts, Huxley, and people like that or spiritual source books like *The Tibetan Book of the Dead* and the *Tao Te Ching*. Mine were literary novels, like *Moby Dick*, stuff by Jane Austen, Tolkien's saga, and my astrology sources. For all our differences, we had some nice talks about books and life. I liked hearing what he'd been learning from his books and from other people in the Haight.

One afternoon he came to my room to borrow one of my astrology books, and I asked him about karma, about how that might be involved in my relationships with some problem people in my life. (Like my difficult friends, Gwen and Liz, but I didn't tell him about them. Not yet, anyway. Maybe another time.)

"Difficult people, huh? Do they keep showing up in your life?"

I said they did, and he went on.

"Well, I'd guess they're around for a reason. Might be some sort of 'karma lock.' Like, you have to work out your karmas together. That can happen. Not often, but sometimes.

"The solution seems to be finding a way to do that, work it out. Usually, you can't go your separate ways until you both figure it out.

"Then, maybe you can separate."

Oh, great, I thought. I may not be finished with them after all.

But, while we were talking, I thought I'd ask him about Jim and Elizabeth. "Not that it's any of my business, but I can't quite make them out. He's all quiet and standoffish, and she's so strong and 'out there.' But, I don't think she really bosses him around. For that matter I'm not even sure if they're really a couple."

He laughed. "Lots of people think she's the boss and rules the roost, but if you watch real carefully, you'll see she sort of checks with him and sometimes he makes a little movement of his eyes or mouth, I don't know, and she backs right down, laughs, changes the subject, whatever. So, I think he's stronger than people think and that they've really got something going for them."

He stopped for a moment and got real serious. "Just between us, I do wish they weren't shooting meth."

"Yeah, I know what you mean. Think it's their karma some way?"

He only shrugged, so I decided to ask him something else.

"I've got a question that's been eating at me…what one of the guys who was crashing with us said. He gave me a bit of flak about the fact that I had part-time jobs. Like how could I be a hippie if I had a job? Earned money? Wasn't that an establishment trap?

"I told him that eating wasn't a trap, but starving was."

David laughed, so I had to add that a smart ass comeback didn't mean he wasn't right, and it had been bothering me.

He told me I was cool and went on to tell me a couple of things he believed about work. Number one was: "Do what you love, love what you do; and, if you can't love it, then find something else you can." And, Number two was: "Any job that puts food on the table is a good job." There was no Number three.

Afterwards, we talked about "life" a bit, and he said, "Think about it, how do you want the world to be in the next five, ten, fifty years? If you start living as if that's where you're headed, it'll happen. That's what Gandhi was talking about when he said, 'Be the change you want to see in the world.'"

Those were just a few of the things he'd gleaned from his books and conversations. Maybe they were a little clichéd, I wasn't sure and I didn't care. They helped me out; I could work with them; they were tools I could use.

✳

I studied some new books I'd borrowed on astrology and began doing the charts a little differently. Instead of pretending all the houses were equal, as they were on the store-bought forms, I did 360 degree astrological charts where I gave each house the number of degrees they actually had. Interesting, and it certainly made seeing all the different relationships between the planets easier. A Grand Trine actually looked like an equilateral triangle.

I did a few more charts for people in the house, and then I stopped. I had to – sometimes the charts were just too eerily on point. For instance, when I did Zander's, I got "death of the father" twice, and both his father and step-father had died in WWII Hungary – one in a Nazi death camp and the other in a Russian gulag. Creepy.

There was another for a girl I knew who was pretty troubled that mentioned suicide. I knew she'd made a few attempts, and I decided to leave out that part.

The kicker for me was how often people would zero in on one tiny negativity in the chart and then completely dismiss all positives. They would have glowing aspects and all sorts of possibilities, but they'd focus on a little thing at the bottom of page three of seven saying something like, "May be tempted to stretch the truth when backed into a corner."

They'd beat themselves up over it, and that pissed me off.

Of course, I did the same thing with my own chart. Maybe that's why I got so pissed.

All anyone had to do to get the better of me was tell me my weaknesses were all that was true of me and I'd believe it. I'd crawl into my cave carrying it with me for months, maybe even longer. I was getting better, but still…

I wished I could believe in Taoism or any one of the various things in vogue, but the most I did was pick up a few sayings I liked. When I didn't know what to do or think, I'd try them out. If they worked, great; if they didn't, well, I could try something else or move on.

At least they had a chance at stopping me from beating my head bloody against various brick walls.

David said that when I found myself doing that, I should step back and take a good look at the wall.

Maybe I could simply walk around it.

CHAPTER SEVENTEEN

When I got home from a little temp gig at the Psychedelic Shop, I found everyone in Sunny and David's room gathered around listening to David's latest stray: Nick Wildcat – a stage name, needless to say. David had found him up at the Straight Theater trying to get some leads on a new gig.

Nick was a musician from Philadelphia looking for a band. He'd played with lots of groups, standing in for folks who were sick or something, whatever was needed. I gathered that he played decent drums and keyboard, sang, and could even do a few licks on the guitar if he had to. It had all been great experience for him, but now he was ready to be part of a permanent band, and he figured San Francisco was the place to find a good one.

Nice looking guy, dressed in black jeans and a black suede fringed jacket. Not a big fellow, kind of average, with long dark hair, no beard, and the brightest blue eyes I'd ever seen. A triple Scorpio, wouldn't you know, and quite a sense of humor, too. He had a million stories about various rock bands, the players, venues in which he'd performed, crazy exploits in hotel rooms, performance disasters…the works.

Everyone laughed at his stories, and he laughed right along with them. It was one of those laughs that make you smile just to hear it. He was positively charming; I didn't think there was anyone around like that anymore, outside of old books.

Sunny had thrown together a big casserole for supper

and after eating he took off to talk to some people. Tonight, he'd crash on a bed roll in Carl's room.

I didn't see him the next morning before I went off to work, but he was there when I got back home. Everyone had gathered again in Sunny and David's room, and Nick called me over to sit on a free cushion in front of him.

Okay, I'll admit it: I liked being picked by the coolest guy in the room. It was quite a novelty.

People were telling stories, passing a joint around, and Nick absent mindedly put a hand on my shoulder when he was leaned forward to make a point. Feeling how tense I was, he began massaging them.

He was good at it, and I was a little disconcerted, and got even more so when he leaned forward and whispered a comment in my ear. Nothing outrageous or flirtatious, nothing like that, just something about a bit of nothing, but I felt…well, something, I guess. Something besides shock that a stranger had touched me.

His breath was certainly warm on my neck.

Of course, when I helped Sunny carry our dishes back to the kitchen, she cornered me. Never one to miss such things, she grinned at me and immediately asked, "Like him?"

I might have gotten away with a shrug, but I blushed. Hard to look cool when you're blushing.

"Sure. He's…nice enough," I said.

She laughed at me, gave me a quick hug, and under her breath said, "You be careful. Musicians never stay in one place very long."

"Yeah, sure. Not to worry. No problem."

I had dinner the next night with Leah. These days, she made it a point to invite me over at least once or twice a month to be sure I was eating. My adopted Jewish mother. Good old Leah.

Anyway, it was after I got home and went to bed that Nick knocked on my door. I don't know how late it was, but it was dark and quiet in the house.

Turned out Carl had brought home a girl, and Nick needed to find another bit of floor space to crash.

"Sure, fine with me," I said and rolled over to go back to sleep.

I heard him unroll his sleeping pad and start to get comfortable on the floor and then he groaned.

I had to ask, didn't I?

"What's the matter?"

"Oh, nothing. I fell off the stage a couple of days ago and bruised the hell out of my hip. It's hard to find a comfortable position on the floor to sleep."

I was taking it all in, when he added, "You wouldn't have some room up there on the mattress, would you? I could make myself really, really small and not bother you, I promise. Cross my heart."

"Well…" and he was there.

He couldn't see me roll my eyes, so I gave it up and scrunched over to one side of the bed. He cozied up on top of the blankets, not quite spooning, but close to it.

"Oh, much better," and he laughed that laugh of his, so I had to smile. He was still for maybe two minutes and then he started twitching a bit.

I asked him what the matter was, and he said, "I'm sorry. It's just that I'm cold."

There was a mischievous smile behind that line, and I

had to laugh, which made him laugh and well...he began burrowing closer, getting under the covers, pulling me around, and stroking my neck, back, legs, and making coaxing wheedling noises and comments.

And, then he was on top of me.

I couldn't tell when he entered me. It wasn't like it hurt or anything.

To be honest, I didn't feel much at all.

I kept waiting to feel something...and waiting. And... nothing.

He whispered in my ear, asking me if he could come inside me. I thought maybe I'd feel something then, so I said, "Whatever you want."

He finished and the only thing I felt was a little wiggle of something wet and warm flopping out of me before he rolled over and went to sleep.

That was it?

I felt cheated. What a rip off! All those years of fear and trepidation, and that was all there was to it?

All the raptures of romantic novels and hot porn and – pffft – that was all?

Was something wrong with me? With him? It was so nothing, so not a big deal and, frankly, it didn't seem to have much to do with me.

Besides, I didn't even get a kiss out of it.

Had I been turned on? Yeah, probably, but I didn't feel frustrated now, so maybe I hadn't been all that hot for him.

More than anything, I was simply glad it was over, the whole virginity thing. And, if he was any indication, I certainly had nothing to fear about sex anymore. There was that.

I looked at him sleeping there beside me and wondered

if we would be an item in the morning. Were we dating now? I kind of doubted it.

I was right. He was gone when I woke up and came back the next afternoon with a teenage blond chick. Yeah, I was a little pissed, sure, but he was what? Nineteen, twenty? What did I expect?

Well, I hadn't expected to be a one-night stand, but it was okay. It's not like I felt I was missing out on anything with him, and my vanity would recover.

Sunny really wanted to lay into him when I told her what happened, and maybe I didn't have to get too pissed because she was. Anyway, it was nice to know she still had my back.

I told her I was relieved, that at least it was over and done with – I wasn't a virgin anymore.

She congratulated me, and I didn't want to disappoint her, so I didn't say what a big nothing it had been.

Two days later, he left town. David said he was heading down to LA.

I never even learned what his real last name was.

Oh, well. Easy come, easy go.

I wondered from time to time why it was so easy to let the idea of him go when we'd actually slept together, and I still thought about Gwen when there'd only been a kiss involved.

Was he that bad a lover? Or was it that I cared more about Gwen?

Then I remembered I had a tendency to over think things and decided to go see if we had anything chocolate in the refrigerator.

Posted over the refrigerator:

The Tao of heaven does not strive,
and yet it overcomes.
It does not speak, yet is answered.
It does not ask, yet is supplied with all needs.
It seems at ease, and yet it follows a plan.
Heaven's net casts wide.
Though its meshes are coarse, nothing slips through.

CHAPTER EIGHTEEN

I dream. It's June and I'm ten again, going out to play.

Chucky, Rich, and I gathered at the Cameron's house in the afternoon and John came out with his brother Al. We decided that the cowboys and Indians had made peace; it was time to be pirates and/or explorers. (There was only a fine line between them.)

We made a map that led to a secret island and hidden treasure. John would be the captain, Chucky the first mate, and the rest of us the sailors. We went out to the old tree fort in the woods and threw ropes over tree limbs. We climbed the ropes and swung from one tree to another on them.

It was a perilous voyage across the sea through hurricanes and attacks by other pirates or monsters from the deeps, but eventually we won through. We landed on the island, fought our way through the cannibals…and, about then, our mothers called us home to dinner.

We swore to meet again on the morrow to continue our adventure. "Aye, aye, cap'n."

It wasn't so different these days.

We played, dressed up, and created new names and new identities for ourselves. We had mythic adventures, and sought treasures, the island of Circe, a Golden Fleece, serenity, peace, and enlightenment at the feet of gurus, mystics, and rock stars. Each day was magical and everything was significant, had a meaning, if only we paid attention, could ferret it out.

Reminder: Be careful how you think of the world – it IS that way.

So, I smoked a bit of grass, dropped some acid, and went off to discover the day.

I passed my brothers and sisters in the street, and we smiled at each other in recognition, in collusion with our joy at Be-ing.

A free Medical Clinic opened in the Haight that summer. A whole lot of doctors volunteered their time and did a roaring business, mostly in first aid, drug reactions, and VD, but also a few other things. Very cool of them, we all thought. More people validating the kind of life we were trying to live, helping to support us.

The cops were something else. Sometimes they were cool and would return our smiles. Other times, we caught them nodding their heads in time to whatever music was playing at the free concerts in the park. They might even turn their backs sometimes on a joint being handed around, that sort of thing. I even heard that some of our regular neighborhood cops actually clued in the Diggers once or twice when something was coming down so they could get us off the streets. We had a strong suspicion that at least a few of them smoked a bit of grass on their off hours.

One day, a neighbor cop stopped David and me on the street and we got to talking. He wanted to know how the hippies had turned the Hells Angels into such pussycats.

Probably a good thing an Angel wasn't within earshot of that!

Anyway, David told him we hadn't "done" anything and suggested maybe the Angels decided we were harmless and needed protection. We certainly weren't a threat to them.

That seemed to make sense to the cop. At least he nodded and went on his way.

I thought he was a good guy, but David pointed out that, no matter how nice some cops could be, a cop was still a cop. We had to be careful, know who we were talking to, remember what they were, and not push a good thing or assume they were our buddies or anything.

I knew he was right. I remembered how every once in a while I'd see a young kid, stoned out of his mind, trying to lay a "peace and love" trip on a cop. I'd look at the cop, see something there, and I'd cringe, have to close my eyes, afraid of what might happen next.

And, when they called in the riot squads or the tactical units, like when some people blocked the streets and started dancing, or maybe when the Diggers decided to put on one of their shows in the middle of everything…that was a whole other situation. Those guys were a very different breed of cat. Instead of walking around, they swaggered, made a point of adjusting their guns a lot, and slapped their sticks against their palms. Like they enjoyed the sound or something. And they never, ever cracked a smile.

Very intense.

I saw Reverend Harris of All Saints Episcopal one time trying to talk to a couple of them and the look they gave him…well, it was scary. Luckily, they turned their backs on him and walked away. I think it might have been a lot worse, and the Rev looked pretty shaken, too.

Man, it used to be all happy and easy walking down the street, talking with folks, tripping, everyone friendly and cool, ready to help out, give you a smile…it wasn't always like that anymore.

※

My diploma finally arrived in the mail and I picked it up in the box outside the front door, where it had been safe from Tex. I was a bit shocked to see that it was signed by Ronald Reagan. (I still hadn't been able to wrap my brain around the idea that the state had elected a movie actor for governor. Not even a good actor at that.)

I was certainly no fan of his, but my father was, so I mailed it to him for safe-keeping. That's what I said, but maybe it was to prove something. Would it redeem me a little in his eyes? Not that I cared.

※

My *I Ching* reading for the day:

> *The best way to fight evil is to make energetic*
> *progress in the good.*
> *Fighting evil just gives it strength.*

Sort of like what John said the other day about people becoming what they hate. I didn't think I hated anything. Disliked, sure; but real hate? No, I didn't think so. Not right now, anyway.

I knew that I had the capacity for it, but I'd had to let go of that; hatred took so much damn energy. When I felt it creeping back in, I tried to remember all that.

Oh, jeez – it almost sounded like I wanted to be one of the hippies putting flowers down the barrels of rifles.

Well, better than picking up a gun myself, I guessed.

I had company in that thought: a few more guys had come to stay with us on their way to Canada to escape the draft that week. Most of them weren't even real hippies; they just didn't want to go to war. A couple had been called up and were fleeing; others figured it was going to happen so they wanted to split first.

I didn't know what was going on with David and the draft, but Carl had flat feet and was exempt. Our newest guests, Jerry and Tom, were on the run and moved often, leaving no forwarding addresses. If no one knew where they were, they couldn't be drafted, could they?

When they called home, they didn't give an address. If they wanted to ask for money, they had it sent to general delivery or a friend's place. They told their folks to tell the draft board they didn't know where they were, but suspected they were in Canada. That's where they were headed anyway.

Sometimes their mothers cried or their fathers yelled at them. Eventually, some stopped accepting the collect calls. The boys were casual about it, but you could tell it hurt.

And then there was my little brother.

What the hell were you thinking, Jack?

He'd quit or dropped out of college, I wasn't sure which, and he figured the draft was coming for him. He wasn't going to Canada, not him, so he thought he'd enlist to get some control over things, maybe get some useful training, GI benefits, and all that. Leastwise that's what he told me when he called me on the pay phone.

What on earth made him choose the Marine Corps when they were getting killed left and right? He told me they promised him computer training, something he could use later, it was a coming field and all. When I asked if he'd gotten that in writing, he admitted he hadn't.

I had to close my eyes and sigh. He couldn't get the full effect of that over the phone, but it was too late now, anyway – he'd signed the papers and they owned him now.

A month later, Jack dropped me a line that he was on his way to Parris Island for basic training; he wanted to give me a heads up that I wouldn't hear from him for a while.

And, what kind of training was he going to get? I asked.

Machine gunner.

Right. So many civilian applications – if you were a 20s mobster.

I told him good luck and decided not to tell him about my move to the Haight and what I was getting involved with right then.

Thinking about how I might explain things to him at some point, I made a little chart with columns for Hippies, Radicals, and Straights. Then I entered single words to describe them.

Hippies	Radicals	Straights
mellow	intense	rigid
cool	hot	cold
spiritual	principled	pragmatic
communal	socialist	capitalist

Fun to do. Another list, another "work in progress," and an exercise in trying to understand the world I lived in. (I guess I was still enamored with words.)

CHAPTER NINETEEN

"Anybody know what day it is?" Glen called down the hall.

Somebody said, "It must be the weekend: the tourists are here."

Carl yelled out, "Saturday."

"No, no – what's the date?" asked Glen.

"Hell, check the calendar in the bathroom."

"Oh, c'mon!" said Glen, "Don't make me wake up David."

"Too late for that," said David, coming out his door with his pocket calendar in hand. "It's the 27th."

"That's a relief. I have to meet a guy on the 29th for an interview. I was afraid I'd gone and missed it."

I laughed at the exchange, but ever since I stopped going to school and working a steady gig, time had gotten away from me, too. Every day felt like the weekend, and Monday, Friday, and all the rest lost their meaning. Most of the time, I could let it go, not get hung up on time. After all, time was an illusion, a man-made concept.

I read somewhere that the Hopi didn't have words for past, present, or future, just for whether things were one shot or ongoing. Wonder what kind of difference that caused in their culture? Must have made it difficult for them to talk to white men.

Anyway, mostly time wasn't important. The women always knew when their periods were due, of course, and the people who worked knew when to go in. We let time slide. Things happened when they happened.

I was helping Sunny throw together a casserole for dinner in the kitchen. She was cutting up a chicken and I was peeling the carrots and potatoes and dicing up an onion (and trying to keep from crying). Out of the blue, she asked me how I was doing, was I okay.

I guess I looked as puzzled as I was, because she said, "No big deal. I just meant after Nick and all."

Oh. I shrugged and said, "I'm fine. It hasn't changed anything. Life goes on"

"Well…have you thought about getting out more? You know, meeting guys…?"

"Aah – you want to fix me up!" and I gave her a friendly poke on the shoulder.

"Sure. How about it?"

"Don't worry about me. When the time is right, I think something will happen…with someone."

"Okay. Just remember that the gods sometimes expect us to help things along."

I rolled my eyes, but I don't think she saw that, so I promised to go hang out on Hippie Hill and maybe go with her to a concert or something, which seemed to make her happy. Enough for now, anyway.

I was usually very regular, but that month I didn't get my period when I expected. Of course, we were on that feast and famine roller coaster, so maybe that was a factor. (I hoped; I certainly didn't want to think about the alternative and tried not to worry.)

But then I started to get sick in the mornings.

Everything made my stomach queasy.

Uh, oh. Shit, shit, shit!

I didn't want to say anything to anyone. (Even myself.) I hoped it would all go away, that it was food poisoning, or something. But the smell of food cooking in the kitchen sent me reeling into the bathroom.

Sunny watched me go, and must have gone out to the store, while I was busy. When she got back, she took me into her room and fed me potato chips one at a time.

"That's what worked for me," she said. "How long has this been going on?"

"Just a few days."

The chips helped a lot.

"What are you going to do?" she asked after my stomach settled a little.

I put my hands over my face and shook my head. "I have no idea."

"Okay. How about going to the Free Clinic? You should at least make sure."

Going out the door on my way to the clinic the next day, I found a new Tao quote on in the inside of the front door:

Without going outside, you may know the whole world.
Without looking through the window,
you may see the ways of heaven.
The farther you go, the less you know.

It worried me; I almost understood it.

But I didn't have time for that. I found the clinic and it was a madhouse of people freaking out. There were people with bloody rags around their hands or heads; others coughing or moaning in a corner. Everyone was waiting, sitting in chairs or on the floor. I gave my name and found a spot for myself.

After an hour or so, I met with Doctor Mike, a groovy young guy with long hair and lots of beads. Nice guy and easy to talk to. One of us. That was a relief.

I told him my story and he looked me over.

"Given what you've said, yeah, you're probably pregnant. We don't do much more than first aid here, but I'll see about getting the test done. I've got some connections. Come back tomorrow and talk to the nurse about that and make an appointment to come back in two weeks. I should have the results then and we can talk, okay?"

He gave me a little pat on the shoulder, and added, "It's not the end of the world, either way."

Yeah, sure. Easy for him to say.

Fourteen days seemed like a really long time to me.

And it was: the days dragged on and on.

Suddenly, I turned around and it was time to go. I took a deep breath and went to hear my fate. Sunny volunteered to come with me, but I said I'd do it myself.

What I heard him say: "Yes, you're pregnant."

Okay, so I pretty much knew, but still…just three words? I mean, even if you know you're going to get hit in the gut, it still knocks the air out of you.

That was sort of how I felt, and he didn't exactly pull any punches with me.

Well, it was crowded out front; maybe he felt rushed for time.

I decided to cut him some slack. Meanwhile, he hunted around in his desk and got me pills, vitamins, and pamphlets.

"Take these pills, don't do any drugs, try to eat right, and think about what you want to do. I'll look into a few things and you can come back the day after tomorrow to talk."

So in and out of his office real fast and I left with a little paper bag of stuff and lots of questions. Like, what did I want to do now? Not a lot of choices that I could see.

I could pray for a miscarriage, I guessed. But I didn't pray and I didn't have that kind of God – one who would come galloping over the hill to rescue me every time I whistled. That image made me smile, at least. A bearded white guy on a horse (white, of course). Hell, I'd probably freak out and run in terror.

Okay; so then what? Abortion? Oh, man – the stories I'd heard! Even the good ones were ugly and painful. The bad ones…well, look what happened with Janis Joplin. Forget that. Besides, where would I find the money?

Give it up? I could do that, but it would mean six or seven more months of feeling like this. Plus, where would I get the bread to do it right? Vitamins, milk, and all that for the baby's health, let alone something to wear, a place to stay. I'd need money for everything and my welfare check wouldn't be enough.

Keep it? Oh, sure. Just multiply all that by twenty years or more. Let's face it – I wasn't exactly a mom type. Oh, I'd probably be responsible, but I didn't see myself as all warm and fuzzy, earth mother-ish, or anything. But then, my mother wasn't either, so what could I expect? I had enough trouble loving myself, let alone anyone else. Someone being totally dependent on me…that scared the shit out of me.

So, no way I could keep it.

Besides, I remembered Carl's story about the woman in labor. Now, I loved my stoner brothers, but having to count on them in an emergency… I didn't think so.

What a mess.

Sunny, of course, wanted me to keep the kid, said I'd regret it if I did anything else. But, she was definitely a mom-type and couldn't understand that I wasn't. She'd do anything to get her own kid back, after all.

When I finally met again with the doc, I ran down what I saw as my options. He nodded and told me I had it pretty much right.

"I wouldn't (and can't legally) recommend an abortion, but I can give you a little more information about giving up the baby.

"There is a place, a home run by a group of almost ex-nuns (that's what they call themselves). Anyway, they'll take care of you, feed you, give you a place to stay, and take care of your medical needs. You'll do chores and go to religion classes. Finally, they'll try to find the baby a home."

Seeing the distaste on my face, he went on.

"There's also a county facility, but you'd need to come up with some money. Could you hit up your folks or someone?

I shook my head.

"How about the father?"

I rolled my eyes. "He's long gone."

"Okay. Lastly, there are private adoptions. You may or may not meet the parents and you may or may not know anything about each other beyond the basics. Mostly, they'll pay for your expenses when you can't work, which in your case may be pretty soon. It's got to be hard for a soon to be single mom to get a job."

I had to agree with that, and he went on.

"The private adopters are usually couples who are unable to have children and have some money. They want a healthy child who will fit into their family and, not to put too fine a point on it, from the right genetic stock. Yes, that generally means white and without any obvious genetic defects."

"I don't know if I'd want to turn any kid of mine over to uptight bigots," I said.

"They won't be, I promise. Besides, if the prospective parents aren't a lot like you, think about it: are you anything like your parents?"

I had to laugh.

"Exactly. Look, it's not 100%, but nothing is and giving the baby to the nuns or the county – well, it might not get adopted. That happens all the time, and you don't want your kid to stay in the system all their life, trust me."

"Wow, man. This is all kind of heavy, a lot to take in. Can I think about it?"

"Sure, but don't take too long. Let's say six weeks. You'll be at the end of the first trimester then. Sooner would be better. You'll need to stay healthy, so I'll give you information on pre-natal care. You can come here weekly for vitamins and that sort of thing.

"Most importantly, particularly right now, no alcohol or cigarettes. And, while marijuana is probably okay, no other drugs of any kind. You don't know what's in some of that shit, so lay off. Remember the thalidomide babies? Yeah, bad news. So, no drugs – can you do that?"

"I guess…I don't have the money, anyway."

"What about food?"

"I just got my welfare check so I'm okay the next two weeks or so."

"Well, I don't want you and the baby starving, so if you run into trouble, come talk to me, okay?"

I nodded my agreement and started to leave, but there was one more thing.

"Say, doc – I've got a question. What does it mean that I felt nothing when he screwed me…the baby's father?"

"Nothing? Really?"

"Yeah. I could have read a newspaper while he was doing it."

He stifled a laugh and tried to look serious. "Well, he could have been very small." He looked at me questioningly, and I shrugged, "It was dark."

"Well, then, it could be physical or psychological. Do you come when you masturbate?"

I said yes, and, after a moment's thought, he said I shouldn't worry about it unless I continued not to feel anything in the future.

"And, by the way," he added, "start using protection, okay? Not just for pregnancy – there's a lot of clap in the Haight and you don't want to get that."

He rummaged in his desk and handed me a couple of condoms.

I took them, but I sure wasn't going to be screwing any time soon. My mind was still reeling from being knocked up.

※

Sunny told me I should stay close, and I moved into the room next to theirs up front. (David had just heard from Old Jim that he wasn't coming back. Contrary to expectations, they'd jailed him. Only for six months, but that was long enough. When he got out, he was definitely going to San Diego.)

A nicer room for me and I liked having all the windows and light, but the nights were long. I kept having nightmares about nuns, jails, workhouses a la Charles Dickens, and little babies running around that looked like me.

CHAPTER TWENTY

I needed to take a break, to get out of my head and stop all the obsessing about what to do. Hearing a bunch of excited male voices in the kitchen, I wandered back to see what was going on.

I don't know what had set them off, but all Glen, Carl, and a couple of their friends could talk about was "getting back to the land." They wanted to go to Oregon or someplace, start a farm, raise chickens and crops, build houses and barns from scratch, that sort of thing. They wanted to be self-sufficient and not have to answer to anybody.

It sounded good, but I wasn't sure where they'd get the land, animals, seed, and tools. And, I didn't think any of them, except Glen, realized what grueling work farming was or, for that matter, what might be involved in killing chickens (let alone pigs).

I could be a killjoy sometimes when I got all practical so this time I kept my mouth shut and let them have their fun talking.

At one point, I did suggest some things we could do now, like dyeing cloth, weaving or leather work, maybe some wood crafts. I was going to add drying or canning food stuffs, but that wouldn't work: anything we put by today would be eaten by next week. Why bother?

As if to prove that point, I found Carl later staring at the spices in the pantry and swearing.

"You see this?" he asked me. "Look at the prices on these

jars. Especially the tarragon and curry powder. Fat lot of good it does us when there's nothing to put it on, and what the hell do you use tarragon for anyway? Is there anything here to actually eat?"

I looked it over. Spices, vinegar, baking powder, yes. No oils or fats, no sugar or flour. And, no instant coffee, no tea. "Not that I can see," I admitted.

He slammed out of there and took off for a couple of hours. When he came back he holed up in his room. Probably hoarding something to eat, I surmised. The rest of us would just have to last until Friday (that was when Glen said he'd get his first paycheck).

Not much in the way of grass to be had this time of the year, either. We had to wait for the next harvest. Maybe that was why Carl was so cranky. It would be different in a couple of months, but now was a tense time for everybody, one way or another. Bad vibes, in the house and on the street. And, so damn many people! Sometimes it felt dangerous, like it could turn ugly at any moment; go from being a crowd into a mob.

Leah invited me to dinner again, just the two of us this time. She wanted to tell me about the latest art show she'd been to. I'd get to eat, and I felt a little guilty about that, but I was really looking forward to getting away for a few hours. I could understand how Carl and some of the others felt, but it got old fast. For some reason, being pregnant made me a lot less tolerant.

It took the last of my spare change to pay the bus fare up to her place near the top of Twin Peaks. (It was too hard to hitch a ride up there and it would have been a very long, hard climb on foot.)

Leah was all set up, throwing together a meal for us in her kitchen, and I sat at the little table she had over against the wall and kept her company. While she talked, I considered whether or not to tell her I was pregnant. She was a practical sort and with all those years she put in as a social worker, she probably knew a lot about resources. But I decided not to. Not yet, anyway. When I knew what I wanted to do, that would be the time to talk to her. I was pretty sure she'd help me if I needed anything.

She'd just finished telling me about the show when, after stopping to taste whatever was in the pot and adding another grind of pepper, she casually asked over her shoulder, "And you...what are you up to? Taking drugs?"

I'd known that she'd eventually have to ask me, so I just said, "Well yeah. It is the Haight, after all."

"Marijuana, I assume."

"Yeah, and a fair amount of acid, too, but that's about it."

She turned to look at me and asked point blank, "Shooting up?"

"Hell, no! Not my scene."

She nodded, relieved, I think, and went back to her cooking. "So, what's this acid stuff anyway? What does it do for you? Are you addicted?"

"It's different for different people, I think. As to what it does...well, I can tell you I don't know anyone who's addicted. It's not that kind of drug, not like uppers or downers. For me, it takes down barriers, makes me see things. Not always easy, I can tell you, but useful.

"I was in a bad way last winter, and it helped me get through it, find a way out."

"Mmm. Some people don't have that good a time, I hear.

They end up hospitalized with bad trips."

"Yeah, that's true. I had a bad one myself and it was rough. I got through it with friends, and I don't think anyone should take acid lightly. Especially since, with an illegal drug, you don't have any guarantees about what you're taking."

"So, how long do you think you'll stay in your commune and 'dropped out'? You worked so hard for your education…I really hate to see you throw it all away."

"I'll be okay, Leah," I tried to reassure her. "Maybe this is my 'wild youth.' I was just a little late starting it. I figure there will come a time (maybe sooner rather than later) when I'll leave. Things are getting a little hairy now, and it's all changing. It's not as groovy as it once was."

She gave a little laugh, checked the beef roasting in the oven, and turned to look at me over her glasses. "Just be careful. When I worked at the jail, I met a lot of people who took wrong turns by accident. One thing led to another, and…" She shook her head.

I nodded, but didn't try to downplay the risks. I knew how easy it could be to end up in jail by being too casual about a joint, selling a tab of acid to the wrong person, or simply being in the house when a deal went down. I'd listened to the stories; I knew it could be me.

Leah fed me well and after dinner she asked me how we were eating in the commune. I admitted it was a struggle sometimes. A good Jewish mother, she sent me home with a brown paper bag holding a big roast beef sandwich wrapped in waxed paper and a couple of apples.

A full belly made the walk down to Market a lot easier, and I hitched a ride from there over to the Haight.

She'd made me promise to keep the food for myself, but I

didn't keep my word. I couldn't do that, hoard food. Hungry as I was, eating for two and all, I still couldn't.

I kept one apple and gave the rest of the bag to Sunny and David.

※

My welfare check came in, and I stocked the refrigerator and pantry, putting in a large store of canned goods as well a box I put in the back labeled "Reserved" for Crisco, flour, dried milk, and chicken bouillon cubes. I'd also found a nice deal on a couple of whole fryers that I cut into pieces. I cooked up the wings, thighs, legs, and breasts for folks, then froze the carcass, necks, and backs. I posted a note on the fridge for everyone to freeze any left-over bones they had from eating the chicken, not to throw them out. I had some ideas for later in the month and hoped the sign would work and no one would bother my other frozen bones.

I was thinking ahead, trying to stretch our food dollars, but what I hadn't counted on was waking up in the middle of the night starving for…something. I didn't know what for so I wandered into the pantry to look around.

The cans of baked beans called to me.

Screamed, actually.

I'm not usually all that crazy about canned beans, but now I couldn't resist them. I opened a can, and, when the opener broke the vacuum seal, my hands started shaking at the first whiff. What a heavenly smell! That's what my stomach and taste buds said. I couldn't believe it, but with no hesitation at all I grabbed a spoon and scarfed it down cold.

I looked at the other can, but talked myself out of it. I couldn't eat it all. (Well, I could, but I needed to share.)

※

What I did was start holding out money from the groceries to get myself some cans of beans for my room. Then, while I was in the store, I found myself pausing at the candy counter to eye the butterscotch Life Savers. Before I knew it, I'd put three rolls in my basket. Worse, when I got home, I put two cans of beans and all the butterscotch in a drawer in my room.

Oh, God…I was hoarding food, hiding it in my room just as I suspected Carl was. I tried to tell myself I had an excuse, eating for two, but I knew from the fact that I was sneaking around that it wasn't cool.

Sunny told me to cut myself a break, so I tried to be less judgmental about Carl as well as myself. I resisted my impulses as much as possible, but sometimes I simply couldn't.

It helped when I discovered that chomping on ice took the edge off the cravings.

❉

I asked Sunny if David knew about me and she nodded.

"After you got the word, I talked to him about what it might mean for the house. He was cool with it. He's so sweet – he said we're a commune and we take care of each other.

"We haven't told anyone else," she went on. "That's up to you. Lots of women don't say anything until they're further along, and starting to show. "

Showing? Was I showing?

I tried not to be obvious when later I checked myself out in the hall mirror. I was only a bit puffy, I thought, nothing suspicious or anything. My breasts were larger, but I was so small, I just looked normal. For now anyway, I was probably the only one who noticed.

I'd lost so much weight over the past couple of months that I'd probably have to gain quite a bit more before my pants would get too tight. And then, when I couldn't zip my pants? Oh, God! How would I ever explain a sudden change to mu-mu dresses? Zander, for one, would think I'd gone stark raving mad. And, by then, I probably would be.

I hadn't told Zander, or Leah, or…lots of people. Maybe I'd tell some of them after I committed to a course of action, but not now.

I was leaning towards a private adoption, but gave myself three more weeks. Then, I'd go back to the clinic and tell the doc my decision. Setting a date made me feel better. More in control, I guess – not that I was.

Ahhh – the pantry was almost bare and before anyone started to get into my reserved stores, I got down to business.

First, I checked the freezer for chicken bones. Good: people had cooperated. The back etc. that I'd frozen were still there and there was a nice cache of bones from the pieces people had eaten. Cool.

I got out the soup pot and threw all the chicken bones in with a lot of water and whatever I could find among the spices that would give some flavor – onion salt, garlic powder, bay leaves, thyme, pepper, and a couple of my bouillon cubes. There wasn't much left in the refrigerator, but I did find a couple of sad carrots and one egg. They would help a lot, and I put them aside.

While the stock was simmering, I made a whole mess of biscuits using the flour, Crisco, and baking powder. After I pulled them out to cool, I went back to the pot and strained the stock, picked whatever meat I could find on the bones, and put it all back on the stove with finely cut carrots. Then I whipped the hell out of that egg, and, while the soup boiled, drizzled it in. It was sort of an attempt at egg drop soup.

By then the smells from the kitchen had drawn everyone out of their rooms. I ladled out the soup into big bowls and gave everyone two biscuits on the side. For dessert we had biscuits, the last of the jam, and tea. Not exactly sumptuous fare, but filling and I had enough in the way of supplies to make more for a couple of days.

I put out the word that a package of noodles and a few more eggs and/or vegies would really help. Someone (or more than one) made that happen, which saved us from getting too sick of the ever more diluted broth.

BOOK THREE

Death of the Hippie

September, 1967 to April, 1968

CHAPTER TWENTY-ONE

Labor Day was crazier than usual, and when we woke up on Tuesday, the quiet was shocking. No crowds, no music coming through the windows, and only a few cars passing by on Haight. Several hippies stood around at the corner smoking weed, while a couple of others turned the corner, probably heading toward the coffee house. That was it.

I'd never seen things so empty. David said it was like when he'd first arrived. The shop keepers looked out their doorways and wondered if it was worth opening up. It reminded me of the beach towns back on the Jersey shore or, maybe better yet, like New Orleans after Mardi Gras. The party was over and most of the celebrants had gone home. We'd thought the party was more permanent than that. It had started well before the summer, after all, but now, like the shops along the Boardwalk in Atlantic City, the customers had abandoned the stores.

The owners hadn't planned for that. A few could hold on to serve the needs of the residents. Maybe they'd cut back on their inventories and hours, but I feared the rest would shutter their doors and look for buyers.

"Don't worry," said David. "It's just the summer people who are gone. The permanent residents will start coming out on the streets again. It's cool."

That sounded more hopeful and the usual Indian summer was rolling in, so the skies would be sunny and warm for a week or two. Of course, those of us who'd been

around a few years knew the sunshine was only temporary...I had to stop myself. Hadn't I vowed to live in the
moment and appreciate the now?

It occurred to me that I hadn't heard from Jack in ages,
and – no surprise – there'd been no word while he was in
basic training. I thought he should be finished by now, and I
started wondering what was up. Just as I began to get really
concerned, a letter arrived. (He was the only one in the
family I'd given my address, but I was pretty sure he hadn't
recognized that I was in the famous Haight-Ashbury.)

Anyway, he was coming through San Francisco in a
week on his way to Vietnam and had a day's leave. He
wanted to know if he could crash with me the night before
he shipped out.

Wow. Vietnam...Oh, man. It's really going to happen.
He had to be scared shitless. Or, maybe the Marine Corps
didn't allow them to read the papers. It probably wouldn't be
good for morale to hear about body counts and see pictures
of napalmed Vietnamese children and dead GIs.

Did Jack think it couldn't happen to him?

I still had trouble wrapping my mind around the fact
that he'd volunteered. It wasn't as if he were some super
patriot or anything. Or maybe he was and he'd been hiding
it from me – like I hid being in the Haight from him. Well,
we didn't have any more time for secrets.

I hated that he was going to war, but it was too late for
him to do anything about it. What I had to do right this
minute was give him a heads up about exactly where I was
living. (I thought I'd leave out that I was pregnant. He had
enough on his plate.)

I was broke, so David helped me make a free long distance call on the payphone. He did something with sounds,

and, just like that, I was able to get through to Jack. Ma Bell's monopoly wasn't as ironclad as I had thought. Trust an engineer to find a way around her.

Jack was cool with my being in the Haight and didn't ask a lot of questions, just whether he should wear his civvies so people wouldn't throw things at him. Okay, so he knew about the demonstrations, he wasn't that blind. I told him not to worry, we weren't like them. Maybe across the bay in Berkeley they might call him a baby killer, scream, and throw blood at him, demand he not go, but we weren't like that.

I figured he was kind of stuck now and probably felt he had no choice. I certainly wasn't going to rub his nose in it. No matter what he said, he had to be scared. When he arrived, I'd have to remember that he was fresh out of Marine training and all the brainwashing. At least the folks in the house were cool about him staying with me, and I think maybe the guys actually were curious about what a real live Marine looked like up close. I figured maybe we'd get him a little stoned on grass and show him what the scene here was really like when there weren't reporters around "interpreting" things.

God! He was thin! When he was a kid, he'd always been a bit pudgy; now he looked like a jockey, just a bit too tall for that. He looked healthy, but famished. He wanted to take me out to eat, and we walked down to the Cafe for hamburgers. The place was its usual smoky, gritty, noisy self. People were talking and laughing, smoking grass while the music played and burgers sizzled on the grill. We had to put our heads together to hear each other.

Jack laughed at the chaos and dove into the two burgers he'd ordered for himself. He inhaled one of his before I even got the ketchup spread on mine. By the time I was half finished eating, he'd finished off his second burger plus the French fries, and had started checking out the desserts. He saw my surprise and grinned, saying, "A marine eats fast or he doesn't eat at all."

Oh, okay, I got it. If you're in a foxhole, you don't exactly have time to sit down to a leisurely dinner. Probably more of an eat-fast-and-never-take-your-finger-off-the-trigger kind of meal.

He told me about basic training with the pride – and a little surprise, I think – of a man who has just survived something really bad. It certainly sounded pretty terrible, that was for sure. I don't know why I was stunned that it was so violent and ugly. They were prepping him for war, after all.

I did know this was one of the few times I was seriously glad to have been born female.

Anyway, we all made a point of not talking about the war while he was in the house. We just tried to give him a little fun. Carl dug into his secret stash and rolled one of his famous bombers, and we handed it around. Jack had never smoked grass, but he was game and seemed to have a really good time.

The boys all stayed up together passing joints and listening to music. I didn't have their stamina, and after a while I had to crash and go to bed.

In the morning, we had breakfast, and I gave Jack a big hug goodbye.

"Take care of yourself," I said. I wanted to say something about not getting shot, but thought better of it. Not exactly like he needed reminding of that, I was sure.

"You too, sis."

There wasn't much more we could say.

He hugged me back and went off to war, promising to write.

Bummer, I thought, waving goodbye. I had to wonder if this would be the last time I'd see him.

David put his arm around my shoulders, and I got all teary-eyed for a bit.

Jack hadn't noticed that I was pregnant, thank God. I'd kept my vow not to tell him, but, now that he was gone, the Big Question remained: the baby to be.

No back room abortion, that was definite, and I knew I didn't want to keep it (but I hadn't told Sunny yet). Since I wasn't crazy about the nuns and the County would cost some money, I was left with a private adoption, which, luckily, still seemed the best bet for us both, me and the baby. So, okay, I'd go to the clinic early next week and tell them to start looking. After that I'd begin telling people I was pregnant.

I'd been keeping clean, sober, and fed, as well as I could manage, anyway. There'd been a little spotting, which had given me both hope and alarm, but Sunny said it was nothing to be concerned about. And, I'd finally stopped being nauseated all the time and craving weird stuff. Whew, that was a relief! Everything was starting to fall together.

Then, very early a couple of mornings later, when everyone was asleep, I woke up with a really bad pain in my lower back. I started to hurt like crazy, sort of like the worst cramps ever. Damn, I hurt.

I started to bleed, more than the spotting I'd had before and, by the time I stumbled into the bathroom, I was bleeding a lot. Really a lot and I was scared.

After a particularly bad spasm, I passed what looked like a big clot.

Oh, man! I knew what that meant – I was having a miscarriage!

I didn't want to look at the clot too closely. I was afraid of what I might see, so I just closed my eyes and flushed the toilet.

Then, I cried.

From relief, I guess. I had to be happy about it, didn't I?

※

The doc confirmed later that I'd had a miscarriage and told me to take it easy, so I took to my bed for a couple of days. For some reason, I didn't know why, but I was still crying a lot. Sunny and David took turns sitting with me, talking if I wanted, or reading if I didn't. I felt protected and was grateful for that.

"Does everyone know?" I asked Sunny.

"I don't think so. The boys are oblivious. Elizabeth might suspect, but she's so secretive, I'm sure she'll keep her thoughts to herself."

Sunny told them I was under the weather and to leave me in peace; I was okay, but needed some time alone.

I was up and around in a couple of days, but had trouble with sleeping and nightmares. Most I couldn't remember (and I was grateful for that). My moods were pretty up and down, mostly down, but both Sunny and David told me that was normal.

David told me his Mom had a miscarriage a few years

back and he remembered a lot about it. She came from an old farm family and didn't hide stuff like that.

Not like my family. I had no idea if it had ever happened to my mother.

I tried to put one foot in front of the other and to get through the time without being a downer around the house. In a week the puffiness was gone, and I was back to the way I was before.

Sorta. Thinking about life and stuff, I realized that in the last two years or so, I'd managed to get myself kissed by a woman, lose my virginity, get pregnant, and have a miscarriage. I supposed I could now safely say I was "experienced." At least a lot more than I was before.

What should I call myself? I couldn't really be asexual anymore. I'd slept with a guy and that was hetero, but it was like no big deal so I was…asexual? What was the difference between not sleeping with anyone and having it feel like nothing when you did? Hmm. And, masturbation worked for me so maybe I was a variety of narcissist? No, they used that word for other stuff. And I'd had feelings for Gwen, so was I really homo? Or, since nothing came of it and feelings are just feelings, was I hetero or bi?

Was it just Nick? Should I try another guy? Or try really being bi?

It all sounded so confusing, and, more importantly, like a lot of work. I decided to go back to being asexual or…wait, how about 'celibate'?

Yeah, that was the word: celibate. I could even tell myself it was a spiritual practice.

Cool. I could dig that.

I'd just started doing a little research on spirituality and celibacy when I lost my contact lenses. I took them out after I started to get really ripped one night – so I wouldn't lose them, but that didn't work out real well. I rounded up everyone I could to help me look for them, but it was no use.

If I held things up real close, I could still read. It wasn't like I was blind or anything; it was just that everything got blurry pretty fast as it got further away: street signs, office clocks, and streetcar names. I was okay for now, but if I wanted to get a temp job downtown again and do clerical stuff, I had to do something about it.

With no money to speak of, I didn't have any dough to buy new contacts or glasses. So, okay, maybe old glasses?

Where had I seen a whole mess of old glasses in one place, looking like an elephants' graveyard of plastic and glass? It was just at the tip of my memory…oh, yes. There was that thrift store I'd gone to a couple of times…it had a big bin of old glasses.

Sally wanted to come with me. She admitted to having a little trouble seeing and wanted to look for glasses, too. Neither of us had much money, of course, but I took along a dollar in change and my old, portable AM/FM radio, and we hitched over to Fillmore.

The glasses bin was still there, and I tried on a bunch of them, checking my vision by trying to read a page in a book I had and then the store signs and a clock on a far wall until I found a few pairs that might work.

The rhinestone number was obviously out, so I chose one with a simple blue plastic frame. Not perfect, but good enough for now. Sally found a pair with black rims that made her look a little older and even a bit intellectual. Those would work for her.

As we went to the counter, I told Sally to look sad and verging on tears. (Easy for her.)

The girl behind the counter wanted a buck for each of the glasses. I thought it was much too much, and I told her my little sister and I really needed the glasses, but only had a little money. I offered her a quarter for each, which she thought was much too little, and we went round and round. She ended up taking fifty cents each and the radio.

It was strange wearing glasses again after all those years of contacts, but I got used to them quickly enough. It was funny – even though I could see right through them, I felt a little like I had on a mask. I guess they were, in a way. Sally said she felt that way, too.

Unfortunately, now that I had glasses, I'd lost my latest excuse for not reading the *Oracle*. It was sort of a newspaper done hippie-style, and David swore by it. The editors tried for monthly publication but it didn't always work out and they weren't going to get uptight about it. Only a few ads, a few or more announcements and a bit of news, but mostly a lot of art (pen and ink drawings, colored images/ washes, and typographical extravaganzas) with some long editorials and columns.

I swear there must have been a million words per page in the tiniest type I'd ever seen outside of Bibles, and the words weren't usually in straight columns, like a regular newspaper – they were broken up all sorts of ways and sometimes overlaid with colors. Far out, yeah, but it made for a really hard read. As if it wasn't bad enough that the text was such dense material.

I wondered what it was about all those words that turned me off. Was I being anti-intellectual? Was I impatient because it all seemed so very male? Like all the editors and writers.

I mean, I usually loved words…my own, anyway. But I also believed that words were only suggestive and really limited. It was so fucking easy to get caught in a logical trap of words that could lead you someplace you didn't want to go. And, there were too many people (I knew a few) who could spin a web of words around you until you couldn't move or found yourself committed to, endorsing , or having to do something against your basic, real beliefs.

Was it all the words I didn't like or the logical traps?

Kesey, Watts, Ginsberg, Snyder, Leery – I think they meant well, but when I read what they had to say, they seemed to be playing with words and concepts, trying to take each other and everyone else someplace. I frankly didn't trust their direction, and I certainly didn't "believe" in them.

I thought it was too bad David and Sunny were so enamored with all those guys. I wished I had a friend to talk to, but I was probably as bad as everyone else – just looking for someone who believed the same way I did.

I couldn't even talk to Zander; he had his own guru, some guy named Gurdjieff.

I figured I'd just have to feel a little lonely and sorry for myself for a while.

I could allow myself a day for that.

Oh, hell; maybe even two.

And, I didn't have to read the *Oracle* if I didn't want to, damn it.

I told Sally she didn't have to either, and she seemed relieved. Her new glasses had made her look scholarly and new people had been assuming things. Some of it good, like her being a little older and them thinking maybe she was smart, but she worried that she'd be found out when they asked her opinion or something.

I suggested that she could always say that she wanted to think about it (whatever "it" was) and then add she'd get back to them later.

I got a big smile. Cool. I thought it was really nice we were getting to be friends even if I couldn't be her playmate.

CHAPTER TWENTY-TWO

The warm days were almost over and we were closing in on the Autumnal Equinox. Most of the vacation hippies had gone, but some remained or came back to join the locals for the celebrations on the 21st.

Over at Speedway Meadow, there was going to be a powwow with the Traditional Tribal Council of the Western Shoshone Nation. For all the talk we'd made about our respect for the American Indians, we hadn't managed to have much communication with them. Glen was particularly interested in hearing what Chief Rolling Thunder might have to say in a speech he was going to make to his people at the gathering.

Weirdly enough and in direct antithesis, I found out that the same night as the powwow there was going to be a big deal with the Brotherhood of Lucifer, the Satanists, over at the Straight Theater. They called it an "Invocation of My Demon Brother" and I heard tell that they'd built a really strange sort of altar. (A camera crew was making a movie of the event, for television, maybe, but perhaps even a movie. Probably depended on how sensational their footage was.)

Carl wanted to go down there and see what was going down with them, and he seemed just a little too excited about the whole idea. Sunny tried to caution him, said she thought he'd been getting a little too into that sort of thing lately, but he ignored her.

I tried comments like, "You're kidding me, right?" But nothing worked.

As if it all wasn't strange enough, I learned that the day after the Satanists did their thing, the Straight was hosting a meeting at the theater between Chief Rolling Thunder and a bunch of hippie community leaders.

Wow. What a mix of energies!

Sunny and I thought the Satanists would negate any of the positive energy the American Indians might bring to the table.

❋

Glen reported back to us on the Chief's speech at the council meeting. He was calling for a "Day of Purification." It sounded good to me at first, but then he'd linked it to an event that was supposed to happen in a couple of weeks: "The Death of the Hippie."

Death of the hippie?

What was that all about?

Glen wasn't sure, but thought the Diggers were involved.

Whatever our worries had been about some of the Solstice stuff, it all went off without any big problems. Then all the part-time hippies went home and back to school or work, and there was room to walk around in the Haight. The streets were passable, traffic moved smoothly, and the street dealers could do their business, what there was of it.

Those were about the only good things, because over in the East Bay, two girls reported they'd been drugged, held captive, and gang raped in the Haight. Rumors of other rapes surfaced, too. It all seemed senseless, random, and damned scary.

Not exactly the kind of news we'd been hoping for. Nor

was the fact that a lot of people were starting to carry guns. What ever happened to peace and love, guys?

To top things off, the establishment closed down the medical part of the Free Clinic due to "regulation and licensing violations" (all bogus we were sure) and the Dead got busted in a marijuana raid at their pad just around the corner from us.

There was all that, but I also I felt like there was something else looming. Something in the air. People seemed on edge, like something was going to happen. Dark clouds were gathering. An earthquake? Something ...

David and Glen came charging up the steps waving some sheets of paper. "Here it is!"

"Look at these," said Glen. "The Diggers are handing 'em out all over the place. It's the 'Death of the Hippie' thing. They're going to stage an event, a mock funeral. They say the era of hippies is over and we gotta make way for some new thing."

"What the hell do they mean by that?" I asked. "And who are they to decide we're dead? Let me see that."

I was sorry I'd asked. Like all the Digger stuff, anything longer than a slogan was a damned manifesto. If I got it right, it seemed they thought the old community, the way of life in the Haight, had been done in by all the summer people, and especially the media.

Well, I couldn't much argue with that. Things had changed, and there was no way around it. Life here, the people, weren't the same as they were in May. But, I didn't feel dead, and I didn't think our house was either. We had problems, sure, but we were still alive.

The Diggers chose Friday, October 6th for the event: it was the first anniversary of the anti-LSD law. They'd have a symbolic funeral to usher out the hippies and bring in an era of the "FREE MAN," whatever that was (beyond being male).

We all talked it over and most of us decided to participate or at least go down to the street to watch. I had my gripes with it, but David thought maybe a ritual like this could really help create a new era for the Haight, that maybe it would get us off the bum trip we seemed hell bent on going down.

We studied the schedule and saw there was going to be a wake around the corner at All Saints on Thursday, the night before, and then the next day, starting at sunrise, a funeral procession would make its way down from Buena Vista Hill to Haight and Masonic,

Carl groaned at that. He wasn't exactly an early riser, but I knew I'd be up.

"I'll give you all a shout when I leave," I said. "If you don't want to be in the procession, maybe we can meet up at the end."

Okay, I admit it: the wake was kind of groovy. I sat with a bunch of people and the Rev said a few good words and then handed things over to the Diggers. They went on and on, like they always do, but only for a little while. My impression was that the Diggers seemed to think they were the only 'real' hippies around, like they were the heart of the Haight and probably the brains and soul, too. Maybe they were, but in all fairness, I'd guess we all probably felt a bit that way about ourselves. The Diggers just took themselves more seriously.

In any case, Friday was when the big event, the actual funeral, took place.

The ceremony started on the hill. A guy played taps on a horn; candles were lit and held aloft. A bonfire burned ready for us to feed with our beads, copies of the *Oracle*, incense, maybe even some grass. (I kinda doubted that – there wasn't much to be had at this time of the year.)

Then the parade started. It was a solemn matter for the organizers and the sixteen or so guys carrying a table with an open cardboard coffin on top of it. A long-haired guy was inside with his eyes closed and his hands crossed on his chest. I didn't know him, and no one around me did either, but that didn't matter: he was just a symbolic hippie.

All very serious for some, but more an occasion for a party, getting high, dancing in the streets, and all the usual, for the rest of us, which pretty much disgusted the Diggers.

All in all, here and there, now and then, it was a ceremony, a celebration, a funeral, a party, a celebration – depending on where you were and when in the crowd.

We had a good turnout. The newspapers later said there were only eighty people in the parade, but there were lots more. Maybe they didn't count the rest of us who walked on the sidewalks or behind the main group in the street, doing our own thing for the occasion, some people dancing, others singing or chanting, all that sort of stuff.

I was at the back, so I didn't see the kneel-in they had at Haight and Ashbury. David said later that it was pretty nice and very inspiring.

By the time I got up to the Psychedelic Shop, it was pretty much all over – except for the girl who was screaming bloody murder. Someone said she was freaking out on acid. It seemed a bit of an ominous note and unsettling, but others thought it was fitting: a lamentation or something for the dead.

Later that afternoon, the cops began what would become daily sweeps to pick up runaways and draft dodgers.

Well, that kinda nailed it. Yeah, things were definitely changing.

A few of us gathered in the kitchen afterwards.

"Well – what did you think?" asked Glen.

"It was fun," said Carl.

All I could offer was, "I hate to say it, but although, yes, it was fun, I didn't pick up any vibes it would change things. David, how about you?"

"I can only hope a seed was planted, and it'll just take a little time to grow."

Several of us nodded.

Sure, give it time. What did we have to lose?

It was sort of dead for a while after that. Well, quiet, anyway.

I was in the pantry trying to figure out what we could eat, and Glen had been sitting around in the kitchen for most of the morning waiting for David to get back from the library. Carl had joined him, and we were all there when he walked through the door.

"What do you think of this?" Glen asked, handing him a flyer.

"Another draft card burning," said David. "Tempting, but I tend to avoid those. I'm worried it might make me too much of a target for the draft board."

"Probably would. I had the same thought," said Glen.

"But, you know Birdman? That guy over on Hippie Hill who flaps his arms when he's stoned? Well, Birdman's going to do it, but he's leaving for Canada right after. He reckons it'll take them a couple of days to get the paperwork ready to punish him and move him up on the list. By then, he expects to be long gone.

"I figured as how I'd go down to back him up."

"Cool, and…" David stopped and thought for a minute.

"You know, I've been thinking, ever since the hippie funeral, that with things changing and everything, maybe we should all stop being so insular, start to get a little more involved with the wider community.

"I'm not saying we should turn into radicals or anything, but maybe we could show a little more support for the anti-war and civil rights people. We could show up for them.

"What about you Carl? What do you think." asked David.

"Well, I don't want to get messed up with any sort of violent protests. Getting whacked by the cops isn't my thing, but, if you think this thing with the draft cards will be peaceful enough, I'm game. My draft card says I've got a medical exemption, so it won't hurt me any to burn it."

"Might give you a few points with the ladies, too, huh Carl," observed Glen.

"Well…" Carl shrugged and got a little smirk on his face.

"Okay," said Glen. "Let's get a bunch of us to escort our boys, Birdman and Carl, down the burning tomorrow and cheer them on."

An hour later, David took me aside to ask if the draft card thing bothered me. They meant no disrespect for guys like my brother; it wasn't personal.

I didn't think Jack would have any problem with it. Not going was their choice; going was (sort of) his.

There must have been a big news day someplace else in The City or maybe the news people were sick of the topic, what with the big draft protest over in Berkeley and then Joan Baez getting arrested in SF.

For whatever reason, besides us, there was only a small turnout of five Berkeley kids waving draft cards, their supporters, two reporters, and a small squad of six cops hanging around yawning.

Couldn't blame them; it was pretty ho-hum.

Birdman and Carl joined the kids. Two of them made short speeches, they all burned their cards, and we cheered. A few flashbulbs popped, and, after milling around a minute, we all went home.

"Peaceful enough for you?" David asked Carl.

"Jesus, I might as well have been at a funeral, and no girls," grumped Carl.

"Well, I'm glad we were there," said David.

I was getting out my typewriter to make a journal entry when I heard Glen call out, "Where's Tex?" He sounded a little frantic.

"What's wrong?" I asked.

"I left him home in case things got troublesome downtown and now I can't find him.

"Hey, everybody," he yelled down the hallway. "Did someone take Tex out for a walk?"

People opened their doors to see what was going on and noone had seen him, so Sally, Glen, and I went down to check the backyard. We looked in every corner and even under that old washing machine Glen hadn't been able to fix. He wasn't there; he wasn't anywhere, but the gate to the alley wasn't locked and it was slightly ajar.

"Do you suppose he wandered off?" I asked.

Glen was right behind me and came to the conclusion I hadn't wanted to offer.

"No. I think…I think he's been taken. But, who…?"

"We don't know that for sure," I said. "Anyway, no one would ever hurt him. Maybe it was a prank or just a stoned whim? We'll get everybody out looking for him right away. Let's go."

We spread out through the Haight, looking all over the place and asking questions from one end of the street to the other. Lots of people remembered Tex, but no one had seen him today.

Glen got angrier and more desperate as the day went on. He kept circling back to the house, hoping Tex had come back, getting sadder and more defeated, until he finally sat down on the front steps and buried his face in his hands.

That's how we found him when we got back later that afternoon. He looked up at us with hope, but we had to shake our heads. "No leads, man. Sorry."

He didn't want to come inside yet; he planned to go out looking again later, and we didn't try to talk him out of it.

It was hard to get to sleep, and Glen probably didn't sleep at all. Leastways when I got up around five a.m. he was sitting in the kitchen in the same clothes he'd had on. And, he wasn't looking any happier, so I didn't ask, just put a cup of coffee in front of him. We sat there a while, me drinking coffee, him staring at his mug.

Suddenly he sat up straight.

"What?" I asked.

"Listen!"

And I heard it: a barely audible whimper outside the

back door.

"Oh, my God!" I said. Glen was already rushing for the door and threw it open. Probably scared the hell out of Tex, but the dog was in no shape to complain: He was dirty and bloody, but he was home.

"You poor guy…what all has happened to you, partner? Easy there, let me see," and Glenn started looking him over. "Your leg's not good, buddy."

"David's back," I said. "And I think he knows a vet. I'll get him."

I ran up to pound on David's door, and by the time we got back to the kitchen, everyone was awake and ready to help. They all wanted to pet Tex, but Glen convinced them they should wait until he was better. He and David left to pay a visit to the vet who volunteered services for hippie pets. David had a few bucks left from the last dope deal in case they needed any cash.

Tex came back with some stitches, a fine bandage on his leg, and a bunch of antibiotics. Mostly, he was a very happy dog to be with his person. The vet said it looked like another dog had been at him, but he was okay. We'd just have to watch him for infections.

Who, if anyone, had taken him or let him out remained a mystery. There was a chance he'd done it on his own, wandered off and gotten into trouble. We just didn't know.

What was clear was that Glen was going to fix the gate, Tex was not going down to do his business without an escort (preferably Glen), and Glen wasn't going to leave him at home again if he could possibly help it.

The house had really come together that day for the search. I liked that and hoped they did, too. I mentioned something about it to Elizabeth and Jim, and for a change it was Jim who spoke up.

"Tex is Glen's dog, sure, but he's also the house dog. One of us."

CHAPTER TWENTY-THREE

As Halloween approached, there were conversations in the kitchen about what we might do in the way of house decorations and costumes. Being the last of the month, there wasn't a lot of money we could spare, so Glen said he would try to round up a free pumpkin someplace. And, for a costume, he told us he planned on getting out his best cowboy gear to wear; Tex would have to settle for a red bandana around his neck.

They'd be pretty cute, but for now I was less concerned about a costume for myself and more with what I might get on sale at the Safeway with the last of my money. On my way there I passed a couple of young guys, day hippies, by the look of them, talking as they passed a joint. One asked if the others wanted to go trick or treating.

"Aren't we a bit old for that?"

"In San Francisco? Are you kidding me? All the gays will be out in full drag, so everyone else will get to dress up, too."

"Costumes are cool, yeah, but the door to door thing… man, I don't think so."

"Well, it's not like we're going over to the Sunset or anything. We can just go from party to party here like we did last year. The Straight Theater is bound to do something, and the Diggers will probably score a bunch of apples, that sort of stuff. We'll have our own parade, people will throw penny candy, bob for apples in the park…whatever the hell you want."

"Sort of a combination Halloween and Mardi Gras?"

"Yeah, man. C'mon…don't be a downer! Let's go see what we can dig up to wear."

So, I thought, everyone was going to be in costume. Probably both in North Beach and here, so…okay, what was I going to put on? I had to laugh a little, I mean, given the stuff we usually wore, how would anyone tell we were in costume? Maybe the guys could wear a three-piece suit and wing tips? Yeah, sure. But I didn't think any of them would shave or cut their hair.

As for me, I flat out refused to go as a suburban housewife in an apron or a secretary wearing high heels.

I managed to pick up some rice and a couple of cans of Campbell soup that were on sale at the Safeway. It would be really cool if the Diggers were giving away apples. I had to keep my eye out that night.

When I got home, Carl was in the kitchen, burning an old wine cork and seeing if he could color his hair as well as his face. He was making a real mess, and it was going to be a hard cleanup, but I let him alone. He didn't want to hear anything negative from me.

In my room, I got the box out from under my bed and dug out my old brown and orange Apache head band, a gift from a guy I knew before I dropped out. I tied it around my head, thrust a feather in the back, ditched my glasses, and checked the look in a mirror. Never saw a blue-eyed Indian before, but I wasn't in any contest, so it would do.

October 31st, Halloween Evening

Some people didn't bother with costumes, while others

went all out. The guy in a suit of armor was pretty cool, I had to admit. Yeah, it was fun and there was free food – apples and candy, as I'd hoped, and also baskets full of free squash, pumpkins, and cabbages. For a brief while, the Diggers even had peanut butter sandwiches near the park.

I'd cut down Waller to get to the park figuring that I'd work my way back home from there, so I got to grab a sandwich before they were all gone. Also, anticipating the possibility of other treats, I'd brought a paper bag and used it to stuff in what I could of the fruit and vegetables. I could do something with all that tomorrow.

Big jugs of apple cider were on a table nearby, so I grabbed a paper cup of that to wash down my sandwich. Yum. The first peanut butter in a very long time. Man, I'd missed that.

A band was playing, but I couldn't see who it was. Pretty good, though, and people danced, paraded, and preened. I got thoroughly wasted, taking tokes here and there as I walked back up Haight.

I saw Sunny talking to Jason and my heart sank for a moment, but they only gave each other a quick hug and then went their separate ways. That was a relief; I didn't want to replay that scene again.

A little while later I ran into Carl who was ripped on something and very pleased with his blackface. Well, good for him, but I had to fend off a corky hug and an ass grab. He was so immature sometimes. I heard him mutter something about my being dyke as I walked off. I almost turned back to confront him, but it was starting to get a little crazy and frenetic, so I cut out for home. It was just as well: I heard later that a bunch of drunk straight guys decided to party in the Haight. That might have been okay, but they were really hassling the chicks and it got to be a bad scene. Fights broke out when a couple of the girls got pawed and their clothes torn.

Seemed that the drunks thought "free love" meant that they could ball anyone they wanted, when they wanted. Our guys corralled them, and when they got it through their thick heads that they weren't getting laid in the Haight, they let themselves get ushered out of the area.

David thought they went over to North Beach to try their luck there. I thought they should have tried the Tenderloin…but there they would have had to pay.

Jerks.

The next morning, I contemplated the butternut and acorn squash, pumpkins, and apples. What else did we have in the pantry these days? I found a few onions and a few slices of bread, then went in search of chicken bouillon cubes. Yes! There were still some left in my secret stash.

I decided to save the rice I got yesterday for another day (people were pretty sick of it) and went to work making butternut squash, pumpkin, and apple soup with onions. I'd figure out the spices as it cooked.

What else? Maybe use the bread to make an apple crisp? Anything sweet left? A little bit of brown sugar, a couple of tablespoons of black strap molasses in one bottle, and a little karo syrup in another. Hmm. Okay for the crisp and, if I added a dash of water, and spices – nutmeg and cinnamon? Might be interesting. Maybe I could slather some on a baked acorn squash?

What about butter? Oh, who was I fooling? We didn't even have margarine.

I checked the refrigerator just to be sure (I was right). I also saw that that the last Tao quote had finally come down.David wasn't changing them as frequently these days; maybe he was too busy. I kind of missed them.

I'd made better, but the soup was decent, the apple crisp a treat. The few leftovers went fast the following day. I kept out one small butternut squash; they last forever, and I thought it might come in handy when we got really hungry again.

CHAPTER TWENTY-FOUR

I was out on the street when I first heard the rumor. I don't know where or when it got started and it could have been any number of places, but it spread like wildfire and by early afternoon, everyone had heard at least one version of it: The BIG ONE was really coming this time. In ten days, on the 17th, California would fall into the ocean.

The authorities cited were professors at UCLA, the *I Ching*, numerology, a famous astrologer, various local gurus, Nostradamus, and the way some birds were behaving. It wasn't the first time such predictions had been trotted out. Rumors like that seemed to come up every three or four years. I guessed that we were due, but it was all new to the recent arrivals in the Haight, and they took it pretty seriously.

I got a couple of offers on the order of "We've got to get out of town, go up into the mountains, or something. I heard it from Joel who heard it directly from Ram Das, or maybe one of his followers, I'm not sure which. Anyway, it's happening and I don't want to be down here when it does. I've got a ride to Vegas and you can come with me, if you want. Just you, for the last seat in the car."

I always said no, but I liked being asked. Sunny thought I should have taken somebody up on the deal. I could get out of town on a little trip, and maybe have a fling. Yeah, sure. Nothing doing; I wasn't ready for that. Not yet anyway; maybe someday.

As the day got closer, more people fled and even the straights were taking off work and finding reasons to go inland or up to Mt. Tam. Some of us said we didn't believe it was going to happen but every time the streetcar went by and rattled the buildings, I wasn't the only one who jumped for the doorway.

Midnight after the big day, we all breathed a little easier.

With solid ground affirmed, David felt comfortable going out of town in search of another deal. He wanted to find some imported grass from South American or the Caribbean, he said, to hold us through the harvest period. He'd forgotten that Joey's birthday was this week and, without David around, Sunny started spiraling down, feeling hopeless about ever being a mom again.

Most of the time she had confidence in David, thought he was up to taking care of her, of everything. She told me David was talking about adopting Joey and making them a real family. But now, when she was in a bad head, she didn't believe in anything and hid out in their room in the dark. She wouldn't talk to me or anyone, got a bit wild-eyed, and then pushed us all away. It was like a bad trip, I figured, something she had to get through, but it could last a while.

As usual, I felt helpless and ineffectual. I wanted to fix it, to do something, anything, and there was nothing I could do except be there and witness it. A killer for me. So, I pretty much stuck to my room close by, reread my books for the umpteenth time, and even tried to interest her in the latest issue of the *Oracle*. If I wanted a break, I'd wander down to the kitchen and sit around with a few people, take a toke of whatever joint was being passed around (if there was any), talk, listen. All the usual stuff.

I was really surprised when Sunny suddenly appeared

in my room one morning and closed the door, leaning back against it and listening. "Shhh. Carl might be listening. He's in his room over there. I can feel him; hear him breathing through the wall. I don't want him to know I'm here. Let him think I went out.

"He's been won over by those Church of Satan people. Anton LaVey and all of them. He's got a dark aura now; I've seen it and it's affecting the whole house.

"Even David – he doesn't believe me, but he's wrong. He thinks it's just a phase Carl is going through. That just proves he's not the One. He's not The Man. If he were…Oh, he's sweet, and wants to be for my sake, but he's not. He's much too young for one thing, and gullible, believing in Carl. No, he's not the one."

I wondered if she was on something, what with the paranoia and everything, and tried asking her, but she ignored me and kept repeating stuff about David and Carl, pacing up and down. Then she started talking about hitching back east to get Joey, about big plans, and places she could go. She invited me to come with her, but when I tried to throw in a few words, she just waved her hand at me to shut up.

So, she didn't want to hear anything I had to say, not really.

Eventually, she seemed to get tired or, I don't know, maybe only distracted, but she went back to her room and her drawings. I went along and stayed with her a few minutes and then left, hoping this was just a little blip, not a major meltdown or anything.

Meanwhile, in spite of all the pressures, inside and outside the house, the other people in the commune seemed to be trying to hold on, and to make an effort. Yes, it was looking promising. But then, Carl lost his gig at the head shop and moped around, and Sally went off her macrobiotic diet, but was still was popping amphetamines, which didn't exactly calm her down.

As for me, I came down with a stomach bug. Had a little fever, too, so I was kind of out of it and on intimate terms with the toilet. I expected it to go away in a day or two, but it held on longer. I was lonely and miserable until Sally brought me some of that macrobiotic soup of theirs, which by day three actually tasted okay and I was able to keep it down.

Sunny got up and about a little more and stuck her head in to say hello, but that was it. I was a little disappointed in her, but tried not to feel too bad.

All my weird dreams didn't help. Most of them, I forgot (which was probably just as well), but a few I remembered. They were my standard recurring dreams, where I'm hurt, lost, or something, and I can't get anyone to hear me or help me out.

When I felt well enough I sat on my bed and started typing the dreams into my journal. Sally must have heard me, because she stopped to ask me how I was.

"Feeling better, huh? What do you write about, anyway? I hear you typing at all hours."

"Oh, this and that. Thoughts, ideas, acid trips. Diary stuff."

"Oh, yeah? Am I in there?"

"Sure. Everyone is and some imaginary people, too."

"Far out. Would you let me read it?"

"Ooh. Sorry, but no. The thing about diaries is they have to be private. The moment you start thinking someone else might read them, things change. I'd write really different stuff. It's not that there's anything bad, but you know how dreams and things can be."

Uh, oh – wrong thing to say. The moment I mentioned "dreams," she looked terrified. Stupid of me, so I quickly thanked her for being so understanding and taking care of me when I was sick. I hoped the appreciation might lighten things up for her a bit.

Everyone was out somewhere, and I'd pretty much recovered, so I wandered down to the kitchen to see about making a grocery list. I heard David coming up the stairs, back from his trip, and stepped out the door to give him a hello. He waved at me and was all smiles as he went into their room. He closed the door, and I could hear the low rumble of a conversation going on.

A little while later, he opened the door, and he wasn't smiling anymore. He walked up and down the hallway a bit, and then came into the kitchen to ask me if we could talk.

I made us some tea, and he sat where he could see anyone coming down the hall. We talked low so Sunny couldn't hear us.

"She's…." and he shook his head.

"I know," I put in. "It won't last; she'll pull herself together."

"You think so? Each time, I wonder. I mean I love her and she's really great most of the time, but then…and the things she says. I don't know what she expects of me. This thing she has about 'The Man,' I mean, I'm just a guy."

"Yeah," I nodded. What could I say to him? If Sunny knew he was talking to me about her…I wanted to be helpful, but not disloyal. I wondered if it was possible and then, I took a deep breath and went for it.

"I think, maybe, she gets afraid and then has doubts. There's probably no way you can convince her or prove anything. In fact, I think that maybe the more you try, it just proves to her she is right, in some weird way. That's kind of mixed up but does it make any sense?"

He crossed his arms and thought for a few minutes. "But what do I do?"

"I think you don't argue with her, for one thing. Maybe you can…"

What could I suggest? I ran through a list of possibilities and rejected most. Well, fingers crossed, "Maybe you should say, 'This is it; this is the way it's going to be.' A definitive statement, you know? And then go about your business.

"You have to do something, I know that, so pretend you've got it all together and go with it." I shrugged and added, "See if she comes along."

He thought a minute and then nodded. "Beats the hell out of sitting around, and that never seems to help anyway," he concluded. "Thanks."

Poor David. Every once in a while, I knew he wondered why he stayed with her. But, why, for that matter, did I?

I guess because when she wasn't in the pit, she was so giving, supportive, and admiring. Both David and I needed that sort of thing, and she needed our love and adoration. Our approval, too, maybe.

It must have been a boost for him when she thought he was The Man and all, but that was a heavy burden to lay on a guy. Would she be there for him when he needed her? Could she rally from the depths for that?

I wasn't so sure, and I felt guilty that I doubted her.

※

She did come around…this time, anyway, so I could stop

worrying about her. And, now I actually had some work to do. Glen came home from his new gig at the record store and asked me if I was interested in a house cleaning job. Seems his boss was looking for someone to clean for his ex-wife who lived in the Sunset.

Great with me. Any money was good money at this point.

After the first week, I got a second job: cleaning the house for the boss and his new wife. A little odd, but what the hell. So now I had a cleaning job every week, one house one week, the other the next.

The ex-wife and two kids lived in a nice little house. When I arrived, all the beds were made and the dishes done, so I could get down to my work right away. I did the standard dusting, mopping, vacuuming, and then a special project. One week it was taking down everything in the pantry and scrubbing the shelves, the next time it was taking a toothbrush to the grout in the shower, but the worst was ironing the two girls' dresses: there must have been thirty of them. I thought at least once while I ironed that any little girl of mine would not ever wear such frou-frou dresses.

Cleaning for the husband and new wife was like being a maid at a motel or vacation cottage between guests. The place had no character and no personal stuff on the walls or anything. The bed was unmade, clothes strewn around on chairs, and dishes sat in the sink. I saw lots of carryout Chinese containers in the refrigerator so I figured they didn't cook much.

It was all easy, they were jobs, and I certainly liked having an extra dollar in my jeans every once in a while.

Just to make things more "interesting," Earl brought over a new girl who needed a place to stay for herself and her little daughter: Erin and Stardust (Star for short).

I was, as usual, sitting in the corner of Sunny and David's room while I tripped on some decent acid and I watched the scene play out.

Erin was pretty. She had long, honey brown hair, green eyes, and a big smile that went over great with the boys. Maybe too great, I thought, but what the hell. The kid was cute and seemed quiet and well enough behaved. How old? Maybe six? No longer a baby, but not quite a little girl. Tex took an instant liking to her, and the kid seemed to know how to behave around dogs.

Erin had a tough story, but I was a little leery of her. Something there…yet, I didn't see how I could vote against them. No other house these days was likely to take in a kid.

Her old man had ditched her. Why he'd brought them all the way across country to dump her in the Haight was a bit of a mystery. She had family in Colorado who might have helped her out. Or, maybe not. Maybe she was a black sheep.

As near as I could tell, her old man hadn't liked taking care of a kid. He'd liked the idea of being a father well enough, but not the day-to-day of it.

At least that seemed to be what Earl was saying. Erin stood beside him while he told her story to David. As he talked, I watched Erin slowly disengage from Earl and start moving closer to David. Fascinating, I thought as I watched the choreography. It was a dance and Erin was looking to change partners.

I didn't think it would be that easy for her and smiled

to see Sunny move gracefully in to take Erin's arm and turn her away from David, keeping herself between them, and in the process shifting the focus to Star.

Nice move, I thought. I wondered if Sunny was aware of what she was doing, not that it mattered. Sunny was obviously feeling better and that was cool.

Erin, on the other hand, looked a little confused and, for a second there, I thought she might dig in her heels, but she got the picture quick enough and didn't resist, let Sunny take over.

Sunny played up to Star and sympathized with Erin's position, knowing what it was like being a young, single mom. They both grabbed Star's hands and went off to see what they could arrange in the way of food, bedding, and floor space. Carl and Glen went along, volunteering furniture from their rooms and, it looked to me, vying for Erin's approval and interest. Tex padded along behind them, supervising.

Well, it seemed that Erin was stuck with us and we were stuck with her for a while. In keeping with David's hospitality, we had to find space for her. At least she had child support money to contribute.

Thinking about it, I had to laugh. Maybe there hadn't been much feminine energy in the house before Sunny and I moved in, but there sure was a lot now.

We were limping along, and Thanksgiving loomed. There simply wasn't enough money for a big dinner, especially after one of my cleaning jobs was cancelled for the holiday (the guy and his new wife were going out of town). That hurt, but they gave me a five buck holiday tip, which was helpful.

Leah invited me to her place for the big dinner with some of her friends. I felt a little bad saying yes and abandoning the others, but I really loved Thanksgiving food and my going meant there'd be more food for those remaining in the house – at least that's what I told myself.

Sunny was going to cook up something, even if it wasn't a turkey. We inventoried the pantry and refrigerator, planned out what we could buy for my five bucks plus what I had left from my welfare money. Sunny wanted to make a couple of chicken things, maybe a big roaster and a cut up fryer she could serve over noodles for a couple of main courses. Sounded like a plan, so we went down to the Safeway and bought the chickens, a bunch of carrots, another of celery, a pound of onions, a big bag of noodles, a can of jellied cranberry sauce, a can of cream of mushroom soup, and a half gallon of apple cider.

We didn't have any pie plates in our kitchen so we couldn't bake one of our own pies, but we did have enough to splurge on a grocery store pumpkin pie (they were on sale). If we were careful cutting the pie, we could save the aluminum pan for another pie someday. Maybe at Christmas?

A roasted bird, side dishes, cranberries, and pumpkin pie: the Thanksgiving essentials. There'd be enough for everyone to eat their fill and still have leftovers. Sunny was pleased and I felt less guilty.

She and Erin were finishing up the preparations when I took off for Leah's.

Leah's son was having dinner with his in-laws in Palm

Springs, so it was just me, a woman from Leah's office, and two married couples who sponsored the art show at the prison where Leah worked some times. Everyone brought food, and my contribution to the meal was to help pulling things together in the kitchen and then later with the cleanup.

Quite a gathering: they were all at least twenty years older than I and very straight (but liberal in their politics). The men wore suits, for Christ's sake, and the women little dresses and high heels. Meanwhile, I was in my bellbottoms and a turtle neck with a bunch of beads around my neck.

At first there were a number of awkward periods of silence. They tried to include me in their conversations, but it was hard to find something we had in common. After a while, I helped out by asking them questions about the art show, and they all seemed to breathe a sigh of relief.

There was too much food, of course, and one person had brought a big sweet potato and marshmallow casserole (the sweetness was enough to make my fillings ache). Most of us, I noted, only took a token spoonful.

The bird, on the other hand, was good, maybe a little dry, but that was taken care of with lots of gravy. And, there were bowls and bowls of succotash, green beans, mashed potatoes, stuffing, cranberries in various forms, plus apple and pumpkin pies for dessert.

Too much food and nobody wanted to take anything home. Leah made them take a paper plate of something and, after they were gone, begged me to take the rest of it, including those sweet potatoes. (But not the pies, damn it.) She had to give me a ride back home; it was the only way I could manage all the food packages.

Between all the food I brought home and leftovers from

Sunny's meal, we had several days of leftovers, and the sweet potatoes lasted two days more.

So, the final week in November wasn't so bad, and there was a kind of full belly euphoria in the house that week.

CHAPTER TWENTY-FIVE

I don't know why, maybe it was having more people in the house or that we got used to eating big meals…maybe both? For whatever reason, we ran out of food after only the first ten days of December.

By the end of the 2nd week, people were real quiet, and we even ran out of tea.

Faces started to look gaunt, and when I saw Carl on the street with a candy bar, my anger shocked me. Was this what we'd come to? Sneaking food? And then resenting it when someone had a bite to eat?

How did the others feel when I went off to Leah's or Zander's for a dinner? Even if I brought food back – did they feel like I was giving them scraps from my table? Glad to have it, but still resentful?

These days Carl was panhandling and so was Sally. David was looking for deals, and no one was having instant success.

I saw that the fast food places had gotten smart about the ketchup and sugar packets, so no luck there. People worse off than we were scavenged in garbage cans. Probably didn't find much in the Haight. They'd be better off over in the Sunset or even downtown.

I decided that next month, in January, I'd save some money for groceries later in the month. Maybe we shouldn't eat so well that first week or so, spread it out more. Easy enough to say now, but I was spending a lot of time and energy thinking about food, planning meals, and trying to get calories various ways. And, I wasn't the only one focused on food.

To top it all off, the rent was coming due again. I knew it was my imagination, but it seemed to come around faster and faster. Sunny told me that Glen, Erin, and I were the only ones giving David any money. The others made excuses or avoided him. Of course, Carl had lost his job so he had a reason, but he didn't seem to be looking for a new one.

No money for rent, no money for food, and people hoarding.

Didn't seem very sustainable.

David called a meeting to say that he didn't know how long he could continue to pay for everything. He'd paid the rent for December, but he thought we ought to know he wouldn't be doing it forever.

As I looked around the room, I saw a bunch of startled faces and a couple of angry ones. Sally was wide-eyed and so was Jim; Elizabeth looked irritated, and Carl looked pissed and pulled on his mustache. Only Glen, Erin, and I seemed to be calm, but we knew we were paying our share.

A week later and I was washing dishes after a midday meal (such as it was), while Erin and Carl sat with their heads together plotting something at the kitchen table. Star was taking a nap.

I was having quite a time of it, trying to clean a pot with a lot of burned rice in it. A real mess; no wonder whoever had done it had wandered away. I seemed to be the only person who, when they found a problem (like old, dirty dishes), felt an imperative to fix it. So, yeah, I was grumbling while they talked and ignored me.

Then Glen walked in.

It was like all the air went out of Carl and inflated Glen as Erin turned and gave him a big smile.

Poor Carl. I was no fan of his these days, but I actually felt sorry to see him so diminished and resentful. I thought a minute and then called out, "Hey, Carl – can you give me a hand here? I need some muscle to dig the last bit of this burnt rice off the damned pot."

A little contrived, but it gave him an excuse to leave the table and gave him a job to do (and complain about).

"Yeah, some people never clean up after themselves, do they? Here, give it to me," and he went at it with a vengeance. It didn't take him five minutes.

"Wow, man. You certainly made quick work of that," I said. "Thanks."

He grunted acceptance of the compliment, glanced back at the two at the table now in deep conversation, and said, "Well, I've got things to do, business to take care of." He walked out with as much of a swagger as he could muster.

That left me with the romantic duo, and as I finished cleaning up and putting things away, I heard Erin giving Glen an assignment to get some things for Star. I turned all the way around at that point and leaned back on the sink, drying my hands, and then folding my arms to watch the scene play out.

It was only after Glen left that Erin seemed to register my presence, at which point, I gave her my best raised eyebrow.

"What?" she asked. "You have a problem?"

"Yeah. You're playing them off against each other, aren't you? Is it fun?"

She started to protest and thought better of it. "So?"

"We have enough problems in the house right now. We don't need more."

She leaned back in her chair, and we had a little staring match. Another time, I might have backed off and let her have her little victory, but today I stood my ground.

"Okay," she said throwing up her hands in what I'm sure was mock surrender. "What am I supposed to do about it? They want to help and Star and I need a lot."

"Choose one; let the other go," I said. "It'll work better for us all in the end."

She gave me a long look and said she'd think about it.

Erin was a good mom in her own way, and Star was a cute kid. Real sweet, but, she was going to take after her mom, and Erin had lost her innocence a long time ago. Not that she was all hard and slutty; nothing like that and she certainly wasn't afraid like Sally. No, Erin looked to be smart, adaptable, and to have her own priorities in place.

She was always making judgments about people and situations. Calculating odds or something. Not a relaxed person, to say the least. She didn't smoke a lot of grass, or take much, if any, acid. Pills, yes: "to sleep" she said. I asked her once if she was doing speed and she was, but not as a regular thing and not shooting up. I suspected she was a bit of a control freak, and I knew she didn't want to jeopardize things with Star. Her in-laws would jump at the chance to take Star away from her, and Erin was fiercely protective. Star must have felt all that; she was rarely very far from her mom.

Just as it was getting really grim again at home, the ex-wife I cleaned for gave me an early $10 Christmas holiday bonus and a tin of fruitcake.

Wow! Did she know we were hungry? Was the fruitcake one of those things someone had given her that she didn't want? Hell, who cared? We needed it and I actually liked fruitcake.

I offered the money to David, but he told me that I did enough; I should keep it for myself or buy more food if I insisted. He was going down to LA again in a couple of days; he had another deal in the works that would hold us through New Year's and part of January, he hoped.

I squirreled away the fruitcake for the holidays along with the money, but ended up taking out five bucks. Sunny was a little bummed with David out of the house so much and everyone staying in their rooms, so I suggested that we go to the grocery store.

"I've got a little holiday money. Let's surprise people with a dinner. What do you say?"

Her face lit up and she was suddenly energized. She grabbed her jacket and my arm and we were off to the Safeway where there was a sale on ground beef.

We got two pounds of beef, half a dozen eggs, bread crumbs, three big boxes of spaghetti, several tins of whole tomatoes and tomato paste, onions, salad stuff, and three loaves of sourdough bread. We also got milk for Star and as a special treat for us all, a box of Oreos.

Lord knows, we had plenty of spices and leftover garlic, so it was easy to put together a good spaghetti sauce. There was also the butternut squash I'd squirreled away; we could do something with that.

Sunny cooked and I assisted. We ended up with a huge platter of meatballs and spaghetti and lots of sauce we could ladle over the pasta and sop up with our bread. We got some vitamins in the form of bowls of butternut squash and a green salad with an orange cut up in it. Pretty nice, but I did have to bar Carl from the kitchen after he tried to grab a meatball before we were ready.

We kept those meatballs separate from the tomato sauce so the macrobiotic folks could join us. All of us made up our plates in the kitchen and then gathered in the front room to eat together. It seemed like a long time since we last did that; it felt a little like old times. We even had a guy crashing with us in Carl's room that we could share with, and that always felt good.

After we finished eating, we handed around a joint of some good stuff Sunny had been saving. Then Sunny went back to take care of the dishes so I could sit back and enjoy the scene. Nice. Listening, free associating, enjoying the music and conversations, smiling to myself, I was having a good time when, out of the blue, that guy who was visiting got all weird on me.

"A writer, huh? Thinking about words to label us? Gonna twist it all around? Yeah, using us for material. A writer; probably a snitch, too. Gonna make money off the Haight!"

I figured Sally (or more likely Carl) must have said something to him about my writing all the time, and this guy was tripping and paranoid, and maybe something else. So, I looked him in the eye and tried to quiet him down.

"Hey, man. I'm just sitting here. Sometimes I write in my journal, yeah, but that doesn't make me a newspaper reporter or anything."

He mumbled something I couldn't hear, and I looked around the room for support.

Carl looked smug, Sally avoided my eyes, and Elizabeth shrugged.

I was a little hurt and pissed off that no one was standing up for me with this outsider. But rather than stay and maybe get into it with that jerk, I got up and went to my room. It all left me with a bad taste in my mouth after what had been a nice evening.

A little later, Elizabeth surprised me by knocking on my door.

"Sorry about that," she said. "I should have said something. He was being an asshole."

"Yeah, he was. Thanks for coming by."

"We're cool then?" She looked a little worried.

I nodded, "Yeah, we're cool. Not to worry."

The next day I had to seek out Sally and tell her it was okay, that she wasn't responsible for that guy, and I wasn't mad if she'd said something to him about my writing. She was very relieved.

Carl…Well, I didn't bother saying anything to him. I was getting tired of his stuff.

Winter and the fog returned, rolling over the hills at nightfall to settle in all the low spots. Cold damp winds stalked the streets and found every damn gap in my jacket to bite my bones. If I had to go out, I hugged my hands in my armpits and kept my head down.

At night, I often slept in my clothes and in the morning before anyone got up, I'd change in front of the lone space heater in the hallway.

Finally, the harvest season was over and there was lots of grass around again. That meant a bunch of dealers in and out of the house and on the streets. And more money in the local economy.

Drug dealers, real ones – not the local, street dealers, but the big ones who went down to Mexico for kilos and the ones who dealt in quantities of lots of different drugs – David had to do business with them all that month, trying to get ahead with the rent and bills. The ones who went to Mexico were uniformly clean cut like David. They had short hair (not military, just short), Ivy League style clothes with chinos, button down oxford cloth shirts, crew neck sweaters or sport coats, maybe a team jacket. They were well spoken, polite, and had open, innocent gazes. They appeared to be, and sometimes were, college boys on holidays with suitcases and shaving kits. I asked how they hid the drugs, and they just smiled and said that most of the time, no one even looked at them twice.

The guys from LA had their hair slicked back, dressed all in black, and traded grass or speed for acid and then spent the evening in David's room cutting the LSD doses in half and repacking it in new capsules. David said that they would double the price in LA and tell the resellers that the acid was twice (or more) the micrograms it was originally. I had to wonder if anyone in LA was actually getting off on the stuff by the time it got to them.

✳

After the latest guys were gone, David came and sat down with us in the kitchen. He looked beat.

"Okay, we've got the January rent and most of the utilities paid for. I'll have to try to do another little deal to get money for the gas and electric bills and more food."

"You okay?" asked Sally.

"Yeah, but I don't know how much longer I can do this. It used to be fun, doing a little dealing, trading with friends for drugs. But it's a business now. A sometimes ugly one. A lot of my old connections are only selling speed and downers and that's not my scene.

"I can't carry things here by myself. There are too many of us. I need…" He stopped, catching sight of some looks. "I'm tired. What I need is some sleep. Good night."

✳

Zander asked me to score a couple of tabs of acid and a baggie of grass for him and Carol.

I'd dealt a tiny bit of acid from time to time, five or six hits in one form or another (blotters, capsules, pills). I'd sell four or five on the street to pay for the drug and have one hit left over for me. I always bought and sold in the Haight, which seemed to be sort of an island where it felt cool to be part of the drug economy.

Walking over to Carol's new pad near Market and Fillmore, I felt weirder and weirder and more and more uneasy. The further I got from the Haight, the heavier the drugs got. I moved them from an outside to an inside pocket, looked around at the people on the street and those sitting in cars, wondering if they were narcs, and if I looked like I had drugs on me. Tonight, I wasn't just getting acid for a friend: I was "dealing" as far as society was concerned.

I could go to jail.

That would not be fun.

I was glad I'd left my derby at home.

I got there fine without any problems, but I did ask them to come over to the house if they wanted more drugs. I explained about how it made me really nervous to carry stuff around town. They were cool, and it worked out great. Zander and Carol became frequent visitors to the house. The boys had a lot in common and had long, deep and meaningful, metaphysical conversations, while I escaped to smoke a little grass and chat with Carol and Sunny. They shared an artistic perspective, which I thought was very cool, and it opened up for me some new ways of thinking and looking at things.

CHAPTER TWENTY-SIX

It was mid-December and January's rent was taken care of, we had plenty of grass again, and I had a tab of "pink wedge" acid Brer Rabbit laid on me after I sold a few hits for him. It was supposed to be some amazing LSD, and I was saving it for later. Things weren't going well enough for me to drop right then.

Rent was taken care of, yes, but we'd run low on food money again. Jim's family had bailed on him, told him he was on his own; I didn't have any housecleaning jobs until after the New Year; and every little bit of food I brought into the house seemed to disappear, almost magically. Poof! Just like that, and Carl would start looking at the spices again. I avoided that conversation by retiring to my room.

Nothing to eat and lots of us were doing that, going to our rooms to sleep, listen to a little music, sit in the dark, and in my case, write. No more gatherings in the front room or the kitchen; we avoided one another. But, with a kid in the house, I felt (and I was sure I wasn't alone) sort of responsible for making sure Star had a good Christmas.

Christmas. God, the whole gift-giving thing had been a big deal in my family. Not just the big gifts, although I was a normal greedy kid, but what I really loved were the little things in my stocking that I got to open first thing in the morning. My brother and I would race each other down the steps, grab our stockings, and rip and tear through the wrappings. (My Mom always wrapped at least a few of them.) There'd be little toys or puzzles, some Xmas candy, a candy cane, and a tangerine. After that, we'd have breakfast before the more sedate handing out of gifts from under the tree and the one-by-one openings and thank you's.

I wanted to do something for Star, but I couldn't spend much money. I only had about a dollar left from my Christmas bonus. What else did I have on hand? I scanned my shelves to see if anything would reach out and grab me. Nothing much except books, of course, and oh, yes...my box of God's Eye materials. I hadn't made any of those in... at least two years, so no one had one of my unique creations. Good. I could make a little surprise for them. I had lots of brightly colored embroidery thread and a bunch of ivory and sandalwood toothpicks for the cross frames. Cool, and it would give me something constructive to do.

I glued the toothpicks together, and when the glue set, I wove bands of bright colors around the arms until the frame was full. Pretty little things. I used the change I had left to buy candy canes for everyone at the penny candy store. Candy canes and God's Eyes – my presents for everyone. The trick would be resisting the candy canes when I got hungry.

Maybe I'd gone too fast: now I had nothing else to do to keep my mind off food.

The days passed, got marked off on the calendar, and Christmas Eve day finally came around. Earl arrived, struggling up the steps bearing a Christmas tree. He'd been gone for a month, dealing up and down the coast, and was full of energy and laughter.

That changed pretty quickly. I guess it weirded him out

that it was so very quiet. There wasn't even any music playing, and everyone was locked in their rooms.

"Jesus, David! What the hell is going on?" he called out.

At his shout, a few people peeked out their doors, but
they looked like what they were – hungry and hopeless.

David took him into his room for a private conversation.
Sunny came over to sit with me, and we all waited to see
what was going to happen. Something was brewing, but we
weren't exactly optimistic.

Half an hour later they came out, David grabbed Sunny,
and the three of them took off, seemingly on a mission.

I don't know how much later, maybe a couple of hours,
I was in the kitchen heating water in the semi-dark when I
heard the door downstairs slam open, lots of footsteps, and
(for a change) laughter.

"Hey…give me a hand with this," called David, and
Sunny cautioned somebody, "Don't drop that!"

The three of them broke into the kitchen, turning on
all the lights, and putting down bag after bag of groceries.
David cradled a huge turkey in his arms – thank God, it
wasn't frozen. Watching a turkey that size defrost for three
days – things could have gotten ugly.

Earl proved he really was a genius: he had a bag with two
big loaves of Wonder Bread and giant jars of peanut butter
and grape jelly. That would hold the house until Christmas
dinner…otherwise we might have mobbed the turkey right
then and there.

He didn't forget Tex, either; he'd bought him a couple
of cans of dog food and a box of dog biscuits.

Sunny took over the kitchen and was there most of the
night, getting the bird ready for roasting, making stuffing,
peeling potatoes, preparing the green beans, and all that.

Christmas morning, we had PB&J sandwiches and each of us contributed what we'd managed to find for this day. I sliced my fruitcake into thin slices and made sure everyone got a slice (and I slipped Star an extra). Sally had panhandled for enough money to buy a gallon jug of apple juice, and we spiced it up in a big pot for mulled cider.

Carl had shoplifted a bag of tangerines. Hard to imagine how he'd done it, but it was a great treat we all appreciated.

There were presents for Star and everyone else.

I think we sort of freaked Star out. We all wanted to give her our presents at once and probably overwhelmed the kid, so she retreated behind Erin all wild-eyed and clinging.

Erin smiled at us and explained that she'd taught Star not to accept things without her approval.

Oh, sure. We could understand. Probably a good idea.

Erin stooped down and said to Star, "It's okay, sweetie. This is Christmas and my friends want to give you some presents. You can take them, it's okay, but remember to say 'Thank you,' all right?"

It became quite the little ceremony, and Star dutifully said "Thank you" to everyone, even though I don't think she knew what to do with a few of the things she got.

Among other stuff –

Glen gave Star a box of crayons

Sunny had made up a little 4-page book of drawings that Star could color.

I presented her with a God's Eye and two candy canes

Most importantly, Erin had saved enough of her child support to buy Star a little rag doll and had tied red and green ribbons on it. Star loved the doll and took it with her everywhere. Tex was expressly warned away from it and had to make do with the rubber bone that Glen gave him.

As for everyone else, Sunny had made up abstract Christmas cards for them on card stock, I gave them each their own unique God's Eye and candy canes, while David had borrowed a sewing machine from next door and cut up a madras bedspread to make scarves for all of us.

There were other presents I think, but about then it was time for me to retire to the kitchen to help with the last of the cooking.

The macrobiotic contingent had returned to form after Thanksgiving. They now worked around Sunny, making batches of brown rice and soup, glowering at the turkey and making the sign of the cross with their fingers, like it was a sleeping vampire or something. Then they backed away from the sights and smells with their bowls and locked themselves in their rooms. Poor Sally; she was back with them again.

Sunny and I laughed. No way were they going to bring us down.

She was the high priestess as she squatted in front of the stove to check the temperature of the bird – tending the offering, preparing the communal meal. Serious business and the rest of us women stayed out of the way but close by, awaiting our signals to duties:

"Watch this, peel the carrots, cut the onions, find a bowl for this, and, finally, set the table."

I had dug out the pie pan from Thanksgiving and managed to throw together an apple pie. Maybe not traditional Christmas fare, like plum pudding or something, but what the hell – everybody likes pie. When Sunny took out the bird, I'd put it in and by the time we finished the meal, the pie would be ready.

David had managed to set up the tree in an old coffee tin and propped it in the corner of the room across from the kitchen. I asked Glen to bring down the unfinished door under my foam bed to use for a table. We set it on top of some cinder blocks and then he sought out cushions and pillows for us to sit on. Carl found some sappy Christmas music on the radio, and the macrobiotic folks came out to join us with their bowls of rice. A big concession for them, and we all smiled at each other as we passed the food.

Even Tex got a special treat – a little gravy on his dog food.

Dinner was beautiful, positively Norman Rockwell, and the smells, the tastes – all of it, was amazing. We almost, but not quite, ate ourselves sick.

For the moment we were full, happy, and content with ourselves and with each other.

CHAPTER TWENTY-SEVEN

A week later and all the Christmas good feeling had gone up the chimney.

The food was almost finished, and David still wasn't getting any contributions towards the food, rent, and utilities except from Glen, Erin, and me. He didn't say anything, but I think he was getting a bit depressed by the inertia of the others.

New Year's Day, I threw the coins for the *I Ching*, asking what 1968 had in store.

I got "Difficulty at the Beginning." That seemed appropriate, as did, "Times of growth are beset with difficulties." Generally, I thought it seemed pretty positive as to ultimate outcomes, so I felt comfortable dropping a quarter of the pink wedge I'd been holding on to. Brer Rabbit had told me it was strong enough that even such a little bit would get me off. I figured I'd let myself fall into contemplation of the *I Ching*, my life, the universe, and everything for the new year.

Brer Rabbit wasn't fooling: it was a very strange trip.

I was there and not there.

I was afraid to look in a mirror for fear of what I might see and what I might not see. One glimpse in the mirror had hinted at horror: blood, flesh, swirling distortions in red and pink.

I was afraid, and I stayed far back in a corner, watching the world go by, seeing auras around people that I could not decipher, thinking, feeling, and wondering about…I couldn't remember what, but I was afraid more often than not.

Listening to music, I heard Janis Joplin getting all gritty, bluesy and raucous, like a shot of bad whisky. Maybe like that Southern Comfort she was so fond of. Other singers were sweet, smooth, soft, tender…like Grace Slick or Judy Collins maybe. All pure liquid tones. Pretty, yes; a nice relief, but…then it would change and I'd drown in something viscous and oily.

Same with the groups, some of them hot, ribald, violent, breaking guitars, throwing things, stamping around the stage, playing screaming riffs, blasting their ear drums out. Or picking out notes and letting them reverberate and slowly, slowly die. Stoned out of their minds.

Things speeded up and then got very, very slow.

It lasted a very long time.

Not just in my perception of it, in actual clock time.

For days after I felt really spacey and wasted.

Ugly.

❄

January was the usual post-holiday letdown, but this year it seemed…I don't know…more so. And, it wasn't just me, either. Everyone was quiet, not particularly "up" and I wondered if I'd missed one of the earthquake rumors. The mood was sort of dead or dying, not that anyone said so – I mean, who'd want to be a downer?

I started thinking about getting a straight gig, a real job that would pay better, but the newspaper distributors went on strike and there weren't any classified ads to check for work. I had to make do with welfare and house cleaning a while longer.

Meanwhile, David came and went a lot, taking day trips and sometimes more to set up/make deals, often working with Earl. Deals were harder to make for acid and grass, and he had to make them bigger and more frequently to cover expenses. He resisted the trend to speed and heroin, but Earl was getting heavier into that part of the business and making big bucks.

The two dealers from LA arrived about ten o'clock. They'd been here before to make deals with David, but they'd changed. Oh, they were still all slicked back hair and black clothes, but now they'd added fancy sun glasses they wore all the time, even at night. They rarely spoke and never, ever smiled.

David told Glen to keep Tex locked up.

None of us thought that was a good sign. We huddled together in the kitchen while the deal went down up front, and it was really quiet for a while until two storage jars fell off a shelf in the pantry scattering rice and macaroni everywhere. We nearly jumped out of our skins.

"What the hell…" I yelled and leapt up, knocking over my chair in the process.

Sunny grabbed my wrist and whispered, "It's Mrs. Gray. She's really mad."

I felt it then, that cold breeze that seemed to accompany the old gal.

About then, Sally came running down the hall to join us, pale and scared. "They have guns!" she managed to whisper, "I went in to say hello, and they whipped around to look at me, reaching for these big black guns lying on the table. The look they gave me was terrible. David told them I was okay, and I got out of there fast."

"No wonder the gray lady is pissed," said Carl. "Man, I'll be so glad when those guys are gone. They've got good weed and pharmaceutical grade speed, yeah...but guns? Man, that's just too heavy."

"A real bummer," said Glen. "Not good to go waving guns around. Not good for the house, especially with a kid here and all." He got up to go talk to them, to tell them what a bad scene it was and how they were attracting bad karma to themselves and us.

Carl grabbed his sleeve and pulled him back.

"Are you nuts, man? They're paranoid...they won't believe any of that, and they might go after you." He let it sink in for a moment before adding, "And us. Just chill. They'll be gone in the morning. If it bums you out too much, go crash someplace else for the night. We'll be cool."

Glen sat back down, and we all waited nervously for the dealers to leave.

The next day, David sat down with us.

"It freaked me out, too.

"They said they'd been ripped off at gun point a couple of times by people, both here and in LA. They thought it was gangs, maybe mafia, and they intended to defend themselves. They even suggested that I get a gun.

"I told them I didn't want to do business like that, and they told me to suit myself. Seems they're getting out of the grass and acid business anyway – not enough money in it for the risk. They're going on to other products, and I could change my business...or not. They could always find other customers."

He shook his head. "I'm not going in that direction. If that's what it takes…no. I wished them well, but it was the last deal I'll be doing do with them."

He looked around at everyone. "You know, it's not just the LA crowd. It's getting really rough even here. It's not like it used to be at all. I feel like we're on a long, steep road down to…I don't know. And, I don't think I want to find out.

"I haven't said anything about it before, but I've heard that even the Diggers are packing guns."

"No!" I said. "You've got to be kidding!"

He wasn't and I shook my head in disbelief. "I've always thought of them as being pompous, but also monk-like… and guns?"

"They've got another side to them," said David. "Part of that no private property thing gives them license to take what they want, you know. They can get kind of hard-nosed about it and sort of explosive, or…I don't know, but it's not 'peace and love,' that's for sure."

We went our separate ways to mull all that over and lament what seemed like the ending of an era. I mean, how long could we keep going like this? Without grass and LSD what would the Haight be like?

A week later, Carl burst into the kitchen triumphantly waving what looked like a tabloid newspaper.

"You know how crazy the straights have been with the newspaper strike? Well, *Ramparts,* that North Beach magazine, has decided to print a daily, and we can buy them for seven cents and sell them for twenty. No minimum on what we can buy. Cool, huh? I picked up ten and I'm going to sell them and go buy more."

Not bad. Pretty groovy little paper, really. Not the *Chronicle* or *Examiner*, but there was news in it.

We were a little leery of doing stuff with them at first. I mean, *Ramparts* had made that snide comment about hippies in February. Something about the Fascists and Birchers, like maybe we were like the German civilians, pretending there weren't problems with Hitler. David doubted that anything would change their minds about us, but Glen and I thought maybe us helping get out the news might soften them a little. So Glen and I decided to join Carl in going downtown to get papers the next day.

I bought twenty papers at the *Ramparts* office and we hiked over the hill, cutting down through Chinatown on our way to Union Square.

The streets in Chinatown weren't really any narrower than the others, but seemed that way. The Chinese businesses spilled out on the sidewalks from their storefronts: pale, naked chickens hung from racks, and the red and gold decorations that seemed to be everywhere fluttered in stray breezes.

Everyone seemed to be talking loudly and shrilly in assorted languages as they bartered, argued, or simply passed the time, while Asian music blasted from radios and record players in what seemed an assault on western sensibilities.

I'd always found the area fascinating, if maybe a little threatening. This was their turf, not mine, and while the younger generation seemed friendly and westernized, their

elders seemed to look at their American neighbors and customers with cold calculation, reserve, and fear. The "round
eyes" tended to look back with confusion, fake smiles, and
discomfort.

Anyway, arriving at Union Square, I discovered a little
corner that no one else had claimed and went to work hawking my wares. Glen took the corner a block away, and Carl
(who had found some wax for his mustache) went down to
charm the secretaries in the financial district.

It was kind of fun, and I sold out in less than an hour.
Some people, usually women, gave me a quarter and told
me to keep the change. Lots of them said they were glad
to get a paper; some even thanked me personally for being
there and selling the papers.

"Have a nice day," I always said, and it was certainly a
nice day for me. When I'd sold my stash, I splurged on a
streetcar home, stopped at the Safeway for noodles, a couple
of cans of cream of mushroom soup, and one can of tuna.
Dinner.

It all went well for a couple of weeks, but then a few of
the strikers started giving us some grief around the square.
It was just talk. They were okay, even if they made things a
little uncomfortable. What happened that last Friday with
the Berkeley crowd was different.

It started out across the square, a protest of some sort.
No big deal, I thought. There always seemed to be a protest
happening somewhere in The City, so I ignored it and went
on selling my papers.

More groups arrived and the Panthers got into it with
somebody, and some Sexual Liberation folks got into it with
the peace people, and it was like a kindergarten classroom
on a sugar high – people all over the place, loud, acting

crazy, demanding attention.

I was almost sold out when, out of nowhere, there was this girl running towards me, getting in my face, and screaming bloody murder. She was so furious she was spitting.

I couldn't make out much of what she was saying, just words like "fucking hippies…bad as the soldiers…fucking collaborators…stupid…morons…fucking 'peace and love'… stooges…napalm, see how you'd like it." That sort of thing.

I tried to back away, put my hands up in surrender, but she kept coming at me and I saw her guys running up to stand behind her.

Glen saw I was in trouble and stepped in beside me. "Whoa there, partner. We're not your enemies. Just let us go on our way."

Oh, man! That did not go over big, and they turned on him.

Not what he'd expected at all, and he made the mistake of saying, "Peace and love, brothers," and they went over the edge. It was like gasoline on a fire. I thought for sure they were going to jump him, so I pulled him back by that big belt of his and put myself between them, praying that being a girl might get me a little consideration. The guys slowed down, but that girl kept screaming and then she tried to knock my derby off.

My latent…I don't know what…came out, and I grabbed her hand, twisted it, and turning her around, I pulled it up behind her back. Then I hissed in her ear, "Leave my fucking hat alone, you bitch, or I'll tear your throat out."

That stopped her dead, which threw her guys into a bit of confusion.

About then the cops roared up, sirens blasting, red lights

flashing, and Glen and I took advantage of the distraction to get out of there.

"Wow, man! What did you say to her?" asked Glen.

"Well…it wasn't 'peace and love,' I'll tell you that much."

He gave me a funny look and I shrugged.

I had a little adrenalin hangover and felt a mixture of shame and…yeah, okay, yes, a little rush, too. I might believe in pacifism, but I really hated bullies and I didn't like being pushed around.

By the time we got home, I was not in a good head.

I wanted to think it didn't bother me, but I kept replaying that scene at Union Square and how I'd felt when I was fighting with that girl. I felt bad about how angry I got, and how much I loved it.

Righteous indignation. I found it…exhilarating. I had to wonder if maybe the Berkeley kids got off on their anger, too.

And, Carl wasn't helping me regain my tranquility. I'd about had it with him and his constant whining about being hungry and then not doing much to earn money for the house, never doing any of the chores, and on and on.

Or, maybe I was just looking for someone else to get mad at.

David stopped me in the hall the next day. "I gather there was some trouble downtown."

"Yeah. The Berkeley crowd was hassling us."

"Umm. Not the first time for that." He gave me an odd look and asked, "Were you ever tempted in that direction?

You know, to be more…more…"

I helped him out and suggested, "Militant?"

He laughed. "Yeah, that's a good word, but I was hoping for something milder."

I shook my head. "No way around it: I admit I've got it in me, but I don't like it. For that matter, I don't like the folks on both sides when they get into it. There's something about 'righteousness'…really turns me off."

"And when you see it in yourself…?" he asked.

"In myself? Yeah, that's the bitch of it. First I get a real rush of adrenaline and then afterwards one of self-loathing."

"I know what you mean. Tell me: do you know the old Native American parable about two wolves?"

"Two wolves? No."

"Well, it seems that there was this old Indian who was trying to teach his grandson some important lessons about good and evil.

"A fight is going on inside me," he said to the boy.

"It's a terrible fight and it is between two wolves. One is black and evil. He is anger, envy, sorrow, regret, greed, arrogance, self-pity, guilt, resentment, lies, false pride, inferiority, superiority, and ego.

"The other wolf is silver and he is good. He is joy, peace, love, hope, serenity, humility, kindness, benevolence, empathy, generosity, truth, compassion, and faith.

"The same fight is going on inside you and inside everyone else, too."

The grandson thought carefully about what he had heard and then asked his grandfather, "Which wolf will win the fight?"

The old man said only, "The one you feed."

David smiled at me.

"Okay," I said. "I get it. Thanks."

"It goes on inside me, too," he offered.

"You?" I found it hard to believe, but he nodded.

The newspaper gig was sweet while it lasted, which wasn't long, but maybe it worked too well. The strikers pressured *Ramparts* into raising their prices for us to thirteen cents each and insisting we take a minimum of thirty papers.

Bummer. That pretty much priced us out. I didn't blame *Ramparts*. It had started getting a little heavy for them, and I heard the union was sending muscle around to intimidate them as well as any vendors. It made for a bad scene.

I thought of the wolves and decided to stick with my cleaning gigs for now.

Sunny, Glen, Carl, Sally, and I were sitting around the kitchen table when David got back from the library one morning. The others had gone out, some place or another, and I think he was disappointed we weren't all there. Not that he said anything about it. Anyway, he had two things for us.

"One: Those pink wedges of acid? Dr. Smith over at the Free Medical Clinic said they analyzed them and each one has a full dose of acid and…get this…triple the standard dosage of STP."

"Wow," I said. "No wonder a quarter tab got me off and it was so weird. Glad I didn't take a whole one. Do you think Brer Rabbit knew about the STP?"

"No, he's a good guy, but there's lots of shit out there that people are lying about. It's not like it was when Owsley was our chemist. We have to be really careful.

"The second thing: I've been reading about lots of plans for some big marches and rallies coming up this year to protest the war. Huge ones, all across the country.

"I think we ought to be in on the planning. While the idea is for 'peace' events, more are 'anti-war' protests and those people always seem to attract a lot of cops. You know, riot squads. Maybe, along with the Quakers, we could help. You know, be another pacifist presence. Our little draft card burning thing was sort of a dud, but there are a lot of experienced organizers working on these."

"I don't get why we should," said Carl. "What difference would we make?"

"Maybe not much, and it's okay if you don't want to be involved, Carl. You could march or you could stand on the street and watch. Both are ways of participating. Or, you could do something else. I'm not trying to guilt trip you or anything."

"Yeah, but what's the point? Everybody knows we're against the war."

Glen spoke up to say, "Well, for one thing, maybe our being involved will help keep things peaceful like. We can try to calm down anyone who gets too carried away, hand out flowers to the riot cops, and that sort of thing."

"We could sing and dance, too," offered Sally.

"Right you are, little lady," said Glen.

"I don't think that's such a great idea," said David quietly.

We were all a bit surprised.

"Look, we don't believe in violent protests and some, maybe many, of them do, but a parade, a mass of people showing up, carrying signs, is non-violent.

"And maybe they do get deadly serious and preachy, and

maybe they don't believe love is the answer to everything, but is it up to us to distract everyone else from their message with our 'singing and dancing'? I don't know, but to me it doesn't seem respectful.

"And, just the other day I was reading about some of their folks suggesting that our presence kind of diluted their message."

There was a moment of quiet and then Sunny said, "So… you think it's their thing, and they don't want us tagging along with ours?"

John nodded and she shrugged and said, "I don't see why we can't be okay with that. How about we just plan to go down and watch, be witnesses at the events, a presence or something. Maybe we could hand out a few flowers right before the march and then step back."

It sounded almost groovy and that's about where we left it.

I think David would have liked something more from us, not sure what, but it didn't seem to be happening. In any case, the organizing and permits would take those people months, so there wasn't any urgency.

The war might even be over by then. We could hope, anyway.

CHAPTER TWENTY-EIGHT

Finally, David reached his limit and called a formal house meeting; everyone had to attend.

"You may have noticed," he began, "that the phone has been disconnected. I don't know if Ma Bell was hip to our methods of getting around the long-distance charges or we simply didn't use it all that much. Anyway, it's gone.

"But that's not why I called you all together.

"Here's the deal: in a commune, everyone contributes and pulls their own weight. My name is on the lease, and I've been paying all of the utility bills and most of the rent. Terry and Glen buy most of the food, and Erin contributes some of her child support money. That's very cool, but it's not enough to support all of us and to keep the house running.

"It's been up to me to do enough dealing to fill in what's needed. And, as much as I love you folks, I can't go on this way. If each of us doesn't contribute at least something, I'll have to give up the lease and the house will close its doors."

He paused for a moment, and after the gasps and mutters quieted down, he went on.

"All it would take to keep us going is for each of you to come up with five or ten dollars a week. How you do it is up to you."

He got up and left us to think about that.

Carl immediately split, leaving the house in a huff, slamming the outside door behind him.

"Oh, my God! How am I going to get that kind of money?" cried Sally.

"What's happened to David? Why has he gone on such a money trip?" asked Elizabeth.

"Yeah, he used to be a beautiful soul," said Jim under his breath.

Erin, Glen, and I were okay for now, but, if the others couldn't get their acts together…it didn't look good.

Carl and Jim made some attempts to find work and Sally panhandled, but it seemed to me that they mostly spent their time sitting around, pissing and moaning about David. Glen and I talked a bit and agreed that, at this rate, the house was going to break up. We couldn't (and didn't really want to) pick up the slack for everyone else, so it maybe it was time. Too bad really, but it had been a good run.

We thought so, anyway, but you wouldn't have known it from all the griping in the back rooms. After a while I got sick of it, all that bitching, and had to speak up.

"What are you doing?" I said, interrupting a session. "Bad mouthing David – Jesus, he's been carrying the weight of this house for a long time, keeping the roof over our heads and us together. Yeah, being in a commune means we share what we've got, but we've all been taking and taking from him. I mean, think about what we've all been through this past year...I figure we owe him a lot.

"And, if we're not going to step up, we need to move out of his way. Let him go, maybe with a little grace? Blaming him is a bummer. Nothing lasts forever and that's not such a bad thing. Change is life, and it looks like it's time to change things. No blame; it is what it is.

"And, have any of you…"

I stopped in my tracks. "Oh, my God. I was going to ask if any of you have ever thanked David for all he's done, but who am I to talk? I haven't thanked him, either. I'm no better than you are." I shook my head, turned, and went in search of David. I needed to thank him before…before things got really crazy and I forgot, let the opportunity pass.

I had a nice talk with him. He was very appreciative of my telling him how I felt about my time in the Haight and how grateful I was to him.

I was really glad I hadn't put that off.

I'd done that much, anyway – thanked David – but all my wondering what to do, where to go was just continued navel gazing. Maybe I didn't say it out loud, but I was no different from the others on that level.

So, reciting to myself, "Humility is a spiritual exercise," I went back down the hall to the music room the next night and apologized to everyone for blowing up. They made murmurs of "that's okay" and stuff, and maybe it was, because Elizabeth actually nodded at me, like maybe I wasn't quite the total asshole she'd thought.

Surprisingly, it was Sally who actually spoke up.

"What are you going to do, Terry? You know, if the house breaks up?"

"I'm not sure. I could stay in the Haight, but it's not all that fun anymore and, let's face it, it's not as safe as it used to be."

There were nods and mumbles of agreement with that, so I went on. "I don't want to leave The City, that's for sure, and I'm not a pioneer woman to go off to a farming commune in Idaho. I'm not strong enough, and I don't have the skills, etc. Great idea for some people, but not my bag."

"Are you going to drop back in? Get a job?" asked Carl with obvious distaste.

"I might have to. Work may be what I'll need to do to survive.

"If I can, I'd like to live with, or at least near, other people like us. You folks have taught me the value of that…that we can often do together what we can't do alone."

My words appeared to be well received, and Elizabeth seemed a little surprised and maybe even pleased. So did Erin. Sally didn't seem to think she was included, so I gave her a direct smile. Carl was looking out the window, so he'd already left us, I guessed. Only his shadow remained and that was okay with me.

"So, where exactly will you go?" asked Jim.

"Well, that's the problem, isn't it? I'm working myself up to asking some people for a place to crash while I get work. Asking for help is hard, but maybe it'll be good for me. God! I sound like my mother! Well, maybe the old girl knew a thing or two."

Glen and Elizabeth seemed amused, maybe in agreement…whatever, it was okay.

One of those moments of group silence fell and was broken only when Star toddled in looking for her mommy.

"'Speaking of mothers…" I laughed and Erin smiled, picking up her daughter.

I said I'd keep them posted on what I was thinking and hoped they'd do the same with me.

❋

Sally came by to talk to me the next morning.

"I've never had a job. I don't know how to do anything. Who would hire me?"

She had a point.

What she really needed was to be adopted. She wasn't fully grown and needed someone to finish raising her. Guys in her position could always go into the service, but she wasn't a guy and this was not a good era in which to join the military, anyway.

"Maybe you could talk to Social Services?" I offered, but she flinched like I'd threatened to hit her and said, "No!"

"I'm sorry, I didn't realize...had a bad experience with them?"

"They'd send me back..." She stopped talking but kept shaking her head.

There was a story there, but not one she wanted to tell me, so I just said okay and took the risk of asking how old she was.

"Sixteen," she said. But, there was a moment's hesitation before she said it, and I wondered if she'd added a year. Maybe even two?

"I've got a friend who may know some things," I offered. "I promise I won't identify you, but I could ask her what she knows...if that's okay. I won't do it if you don't want me to."

I got her permission and went to see Leah, who told me the kid was pretty much screwed. Not her word, but the conclusion I drew.

"Unless," she started to say and stopped to think a minute. "It's only a maybe, but if she had a legal guardian, she might be able to stay here in California. Otherwise, the authorities would have to send her back home.

"Getting a guardian would entail finding someone willing and acceptable to the court, and then there'd be a need for some money for the legal fees and actions. And…I'm sorry, but there's no guarantee the court wouldn't send her home, anyway. Your friend is in a rough spot."

Not the kind of news I wanted to take back. When I sat Sally down and told her what I'd learned, the hopeful look she'd started out with changed to…I wasn't sure what. Some mix of desperation, pleading, fear? Did she want me to do something? I didn't have anything left to offer.

Anyway, by the time I finished, she just looked a bit blank. I said I was sorry, but that seemed a bit lame, and she left without a word.

A couple of days later, she came into the kitchen to tell us that she'd talked to people in a house over on Waller, and they were going to take her in. I wished that she looked happier about it, but mostly she seemed resigned. Since she didn't elaborate, we all congratulated her and didn't ask too closely about the arrangement.

Elizabeth popped into my room a day later wanting me to teach her how to ask questions of the *I Ching*. I taught her about throwing the coins six times and adding up values and then how to find interpretations in the book.

I left her to it and went to make tea for us. When I got back she had a question about what one of her changing lines in the *I Ching* reading meant.

"Well, it sounds to me like going forward, maybe north, would prove beneficial, but not without overcoming obstacles." She seemed satisfied with that, wrote down a few things on her pad of paper, thanked me, and left.

At least that was something positive, I thought, as I took

the cups back to the kitchen. I'd like to be friends with her and leave on good terms.

I was just putting the cups in the sink when Glen walked in, his face and shirt covered in blood.

"Jesus, Glen! What the hell happened to you? Get hit by a car? No, don't talk. I'll get a couple of ice cubes for your… it's just your nose, isn't it?" He nodded.

It was bleeding like crazy, of course, but he didn't need any stitching up, so I wrapped the ice in a clean dish towel for him to hold on his nose and put his shirt in cold water to soak.

After he got things under control, he managed to mumble some words.

"No car. Worse. There was this guy…freaking out…in front of the *Oracle*. Don't know what he was on…meth? STP? A pink wedge? I don't know. Anyhow, real paranoid… and no one helping him…so I thought I'd try to talk him down.

"He belted me a good one, and started screaming bloody murder. Called me a fascist, that sort of thing…Tex was barking and growling, wanting to protect me, so I moved away…didn't want him to get in trouble, bite the guy or anything. He sure wanted to."

"Nobody helped you or the guy freaking out?"

"Nope. A couple of guys were there, leaning against the wall, laughing…like it was a show or something…Hard to believe." He shook his head and winced.

"Wouldn't have been like that a year ago," I observed. "Okay, let's see how your nose is doing…Oh, good. It looks better than I thought it would. Doesn't seem to be broken and it's pretty much stopped bleeding. I think you'll be okay."

As I cleaned up afterwards, I thought about my future.

Glen's story was yet another bad scene. I kept getting the same message…hell, we all were: The Haight was getting ugly.

What was I going to do if the place folded?

What would I do without an address?

Without a phone number or an address, how could I ever find a job? Where could my welfare check be mailed?

What would I do without Sunny, David, and Glen…the whole gang?

Oh, man. Not happy topics for my bedtime, that was for sure.

I'm dreaming, I think.

On a boat, on a river. A canoe, perhaps?

A voice behind me, soft. Female?

"Go."

I look around, but there's no one there.

"Who is that?" I call out.

No one responds.

I suddenly have a paddle in my hands.

But the current is swift; I can't go back.

Ahead, I see the water turning white;

I hear the sound of it on rocks.

Lots of rocks. Big ones.

If I do nothing, I'll be swept into them.

I see a patch of quieter water on my right and head for it.

The voice behind me, says "Yes, go, go…"

I woke up and looked around. That was weird. Was it my unconscious? That voice – a waking dream? Did it really matter?

I shook my rattling head. Whether it was confirmation from the universe or only my unconscious, it was something, so, I let it tip me over the edge. I'd stop drifting; stop looking for an answer written in gold; and do...whatever.

I suddenly remembered a poem from long ago. The last line was, "Most any decision is better than none."

Now the question was – Where will I start?

I waited and got nothing.

Well, damn. I guess I couldn't expect the universe to do everything for me. I'd have to talk to Zander. At least that would be a beginning.

February 1968

I thought it was just me, obsessing about all that stuff all the time, but there was more going on in the Haight.

The next day the air was funny, the atmosphere uneasy. The sky wasn't the yellow it gets before a tornado, but it felt a bit like that. There was a jangling "off-ness" that made things worse because everything seemed otherwise so normal. I thought, maybe this is what birds feel before an earthquake. Not a pleasant thought in San Francisco, but no one was talking about the Big One.

I tried to shrug it off and failed.

Later, I decided I was simply feeling the beginning of the day's disruptions, becoming a part of it in my irritability and anxiety.

I went to the Safeway around noon to see what I could get for $3.55. I was sick of rice and tuna casserole, so I got two cans of Franco American Mac and Cheese, a couple of cans of stewed tomatoes, three onions, and a pound of beef chuck. I wanted to cook up a batch of what I called my "Bulgarian Goulash."

It wasn't really Bulgarian, but who knew what Bulgarians cooked or if they even had a "goulash."

Anyway, there were more people on the streets than usual. Not as many as in the summer, of course, but still a good number. The atmosphere wasn't the old stoned, carefree vibe; it was getting weird, almost electric.

The tourists started to act aggressively and used their cars to shove a way through the streets. A number of hippies got pissed and began pounding on the cars and yelling at the drivers.

I tried to stay away from that scene but got hassled by panhandlers who tried to hit on me for my groceries. I kept saying, "Sorry man, this is for my house." Over and over.

The usual dealers were out on the streets, too, even Max, who was notorious for burning people with capsules of dried milk and blotters with food coloring on them. "Don't try to sell me your crap!" I said to him. "It's bad enough you burn the straights."

It was like that up and down the street and sidewalks – edgy and ugly.

All the energy out there…and around 1:00 the cop cars started to appear. Some people must have blocked the street because all the traffic stopped dead. The drivers down where I was looked a little scared, trapped in their cars and all.

The cops must have been waiting for something to happen because – Bam! – a whole mess of them arrived and were all over the place, moving up and down the sidewalks, hitting people with their sticks, shoving them, chasing folks every which way. I ran into the Straight Theater to get off the street and they came in right after me and chased us all out. I kept trying to get over to Waller and off the Haight, but I was getting pushed and bumped. I felt like the ball in a pinball nightmare.

I saw a girl go down, her head bloody and the cops didn't stop hitting her, so I knew it wasn't safe for me, either. People were screaming and yelling, there were whistles and sirens, and some sounds I didn't want to think about. I saw smoke up the block, thought maybe it was a fire at first. Then, getting a whiff, I knew it was tear gas.

About then, I fell over a bike and bounced against a wall trying to stay out of the way. I got scraped up a bit and my bag of groceries broke and spilled all over. I was able to grab two of the cans, an onion, and the meat. I stuffed them in my pockets and my Wells Fargo bag before I had to give it up and get out of there.

I saw that the cops were coming in waves, so I hid behind the trash cans in an alley, waited until a line went by, and then shot out of there and up a side street to Waller. From there I could see that the cops were massed up at the corner of Masonic.

Oh, great! It looked like they had their headquarters right in front of our house.

I edged along, close to the buildings, and ducked behind parked cars until I got to All Saints where the Rev let me come in and go over the fence in the back to the yard behind our house.

When I got up the back steps, before I could say a word, Glen called me to the front room. "Stay back against the wall so they can't see you. More of them are coming all the time and getting their orders from over there," he pointed out the window.

Oh, yeah. Lots of men in blue, cop cars driving up

fast to congregate at the corner. The cops seemed to move purposefully, but also randomly, like they were unsure of their destinations, didn't know exactly what they were to do, but wanted to look strong. They hefted their night sticks, checked their guns, and strode down Masonic towards Haight in groups.

Edward Bear, the DJ for KMPX, sent us cautionary words over the airways: "Stay cool, be careful, something's going down."

I watched as the others came in and drifted to the front of the house to join us, mesmerized by the show below. So unreal; I half expected to see movie cameras and make-up people, but the only cameras were those held by reporters hurrying to keep up and being waved away.

Carl kept muttering, "Oh, man! They're going to kill somebody."

Sunny was ashen. "David is out there."

Glen had Tex in his arms; the little dog was really stirred up and whining.

About ten minutes later we heard the sound of rapid footsteps coming up the back way and braced ourselves against the walls in a pack, wide-eyed with fear, expecting the cops. But it was only David bursting in, panting.

"They're beating people up. There were a couple of us hanging out by the *Oracle* and they chased us inside, whaling away at anyone they could get close to. Then we got chased out again.

"People were bleeding and on the ground and they kept on hitting them. I saw Dr. Mike try to help a guy and the cops threatened him, too. They knew he was a doctor and just didn't give a damn.

"Can you see anything from here?" he asked.

I pointed out the window, "That's their headquarters."

"Really? Holy shit!" he said looking out the window. "You can see everything. And…" he pulled back from the window, "they can see us, too."

Just then KMPX started playing the Buffalo Springfield song, "For What it's Worth." Over and over. We all flashed on the phrases about "There's a man with a gun over there" and "What a field day for the heat, a thousand people in the street…."

Yeah, man. That's what it looked like.

At this point, we were all standing a few feet back from the windows, so we could see but, hopefully, not be seen. Cops in small groups would come running up Masonic to report to their commanders, I guess, and take a break. They'd grab a cup of coffee and start talking to the others, telling stories of their fights down on Haight, no doubt, gesturing excitedly, and making hitting motions with their sticks.

Carl suggested we open the window and blast the radio at them. We all turned to see who this lunatic was, and David told him, "You want to get into it with them, go out the back way and have fun down there. You're not involving the house."

Carl's bravado collapsed. "I was just saying…" and he backed away grumbling to himself.

I don't know how long it lasted, probably nowhere near as long as it seemed, but eventually the police got into their cars and trucks and began peeling away until the streets were quiet and empty once more.

If anyone had any doubts about the direction the Haight was heading before, they were gone now. Lots of the old hippies made immediate plans to leave, get out, and get away from all the violence in the Haight and, for that matter, from all the cities around the country where the race riots and anti-war demonstrations seemed to be coming down almost daily.

We knew we had to go, too, but we all had the same questions:

Where would we go?

What would we do?

A white envelope with red and white stripes around the border and a red dragon in a corner arrived for me from Vietnam.

Dear Sis –

The last time I tried to write you, I got about one page written and had to put it down for a minute to do something. When I got back, there was a big hole in the ground where I'd been sitting. We never know when things are going to get hairy around here.

That Tet offensive was really bad, but so far so good for me. I'm crossing off the days left on my tour of duty. Slowly, but surely they add up. A second looey was around the other day trying to get guys to re-up. Almost got himself fragged – you'd have to be crazy to do that.

I can't say much about where I am or what we're doing. Probably just as well. I'd freak you out.

So, how are you doing? Still being a hippie? From your last letter, it sounds a little crazy there, but you seem okay.

Mother keeps sending me socks and cookies. Did

she tell you she sends the boxes packed full of pop-corn to keep things from getting broken? Makes me popular with the guys on mail day.

What I could really use are more tapes – like Coun-try Joe's latest – whatever it is. And, the louder the music, the better. Something to drown out the…well, never mind that.

Keep writing even if I don't always have the energy to get back to you. I appreciate your letters. Hope you understand. – Love, Jack

Yeah; it was a little crazy here.

I still hadn't talked to Zander. He was out of town, visit-ing his brother, but I'd see him soon. What would I say to him? I had so many questions, so many decisions to make. When in doubt…I decided to drop acid again. Not any more of that pink wedge, thank you. I got a nice mellow yellow dot tab.

When I came on, I found darkness in and around me. Electricity, tension, violence in the air. Ugliness.

I could only pretend so long. Should I, could I run? Hide? Stay quiet? Fight?

Was I not seeing the exit, a way out, because I was so focused on what was in front of me?

Was there something beyond my so very human visual limits?

Could I walk around this wall?

Tex stayed with me, snuggling by my side, or resting

his head on my knee. He was such a comfort. Good dog.

I tried throwing the coins for the *I Ching* and got "Youthful Folly" –

> *It is not I who seek the young fool;*
> *the young fool seeks me.*
> *At the first oracle I inform him,*
> *if he asks two or three times, it is importunity.*
> *If he importunes, I give him no information.*

Well, that'll teach me.

Okay. I'd stop writing scripts in my head for what I might say and how Zander might respond. I needed to listen first. And then be patient. Damn.

I stayed in my room contemplating all that for a couple of days, and then Sunny came in looking really upset.

"David's going to dump me, I just know it."

"What? Don't be silly."

"No, no. He's up to something. He's gone all the time and when he's here, he's been sneaking around, says he's making phone calls, but he won't tell me about them. He used to talk to me about everything, but after…well, I think he's disgusted with me and my moods and he's…"

She was working herself into a real lather. She started to cry, sob really, and mumbled things about him really being the "One," and she'd doubted him and now she was being punished and it was too late, and she'd lost everything, and…

There wasn't much I could say to reassure her except that I didn't believe he was going to dump her. Not very useful, I'm afraid, so I added I thought he was a little preoccupied about the house, what with no one working and all. That seemed to help a bit; at least it gave her something else to blame.

CHAPTER TWENTY-NINE

David went down to LA for a week. Two days after he left, Sunny emerged from her room with new determination and called a house meeting in the music room.

"It's time to purify and cleanse the house. I did a cleansing back east, so I know how, and, with all the things that have been coming down lately…well, you know as well as I do, that there's a lot of bad energy in the Haight. It wasn't good before the cop riot and it hasn't got any better since. Who knows what kind of evil seeped into the house when they were right out there, in front of the house."

"Yeah," said Sally. "That was really scary stuff."

"So, what do you think we should do?" asked Erin.

"The first thing we need to do is get the place spotlessly clean. I'll collect all the things for a purification rite and Terry has volunteered to help me clean all the common areas.

That was news to me, but I didn't give it away.

"I'm going to need everyone's help getting all our individual rooms clean. A really thorough job would mean washing the windows, dusting, damp mopping floors, doing laundry, the works. Sounds like a lot, but it's only one room – I don't see it taking more than an hour or two, but, obviously, it's up to you how effective the purification will be."

Carl gave a little derisive snort, and Sunny turned to raise her eyebrows at him.

"Nothing," he said. It's just that you women don't have

that kind of power, not over the stuff that's out there."
Under his breath, he muttered, "house cleaning" and
shook his head.

Sunny gave him a long look, long enough to make him
uncomfortable, before she turned her back on him and
went on.

"Day after tomorrow, Friday afternoon, we'll do it." She
laughed before she added, "And, you might want to go down
to the park then. We'll smudge the hell – literally – out of
the place, and the smoke might get heavy."

"Better alert the fire department," suggested Glen. "Last
week they turned out in force at Joe's place when he cooked
hamburgers on the hibachi out on his fire escape."

"Good idea. Anything else?" There wasn't.

"Okay then."

Two days later, my room was spotless and so was Sunny's.
I didn't know how much the others had done in theirs, but
I was pretty sure Carl hadn't bothered. I wasn't sure how
much that was general pissiness on his part or the fact that
he had a new girlfriend and had other places to be.

He hadn't introduced her to any of us, but Glen said he
thought she might be involved with the black magic crowd.
Some of the things Carl said to him kind of suggested that.
(He'd had to brag about his new girl to Glen, of course, show
him he was doing well, that kind of stuff.) Glen thought she
was involved with LaVey.

Whatever her story was, she made Carl feel important.

Anyway…Sunny and I discussed how to clean the
common areas, who would do what. I got the kitchen and
hallway, while she took the bathroom and stairs. Luckily,

it wasn't as bad as we'd thought. The stove and refrigerator were a mess, but I got off most of the grime and what was baked on in the oven was at least sterilized by heat.

In the afternoon we went over what she would need for the rituals and I got a little shopping list: lemons from the grocery store, a gallon of distilled water, a couple of wrought iron nails and strike-anywhere matches from the hardware store.

She was getting four sage smudge sticks. She thought we'd only need two, but wanted to have a couple of spares on hand. Also, votive candles at one of the psychedelic shops. She borrowed my old compass that I'd been carrying around so she could find the house orientation points, and asked me to also pick up four shiny new copper pennies. She also borrowed David's big abalone shell to help with the smudging in some way.

That evening she went out to see if she could find the right kind of feathers and came back with four of them, two white feathers, barred with dark brown and two black-tipped white feathers. I still had embroidery thread left over from making God's Eyes, and she took a bright green spool to make a couple of feather bundles.

Preparations made, everyone out of the house, and our box of supplies on the front steps: we were ready.

"Okay," Sunny said, "here we go," and she opened the door.

"I want you to walk clockwise through the house and open every drawer, cabinet, and closet at least an inch. I'm going to the kitchen to cook the lemons."

I felt a little uncomfortable walking into people's rooms and opening the drawers and closets. I didn't want to be nosy but, as expected, Carl's room was a mess. Surprisingly, Sally's was very neat. Then I remembered – she'd probably taken some speed to get it done. Glen's was a bit Spartan, but showed Erin and Star's presence with a small blanket on the bed.

Meanwhile, Sunny sliced the lemons into a big pot of water on the stove and added a little salt to the brew. When it was boiling, she took it off the fire to cool a bit.

By the time I was finished and joined her in the kitchen, it was ready to go. We dipped clean dish cloths into the solution and wiped off all the large surfaces we could find, while repeating over and over again, "Everything touched by this brew is cleansed."

When we were done with that, I held a bowl of the lemon brew and followed her around the house as she dipped in a finger and traced pentacles onto each window and mirror. Then we made another circuit to pour a table-spoon or so down the drain of every sink, tub, or toilet.

We took few minutes at that point to sit on the steps and take in the sun while everything dried.

Then, it was candles and pennies time. Using my com-pass, we determined the cardinal points of the house and hid a penny as close as possible to North, South, East, and West, wherever they might be. Under a rug, in the bottom of a drawer, in the corner of a closet shelf, whatever. Then we placed a votive candle on a plate in the approximate center of each room and the hallway. Making another clockwise circuit, we lit each candle.

"It's time for the smudging," said Sunny, and I followed her back down to the front door, where she held the two white sage smudge sticks over the abalone shell as she lit them. When they were both smoking well, she handed one to me along with a feather bundle and she took the other set. Sunny walked up the steps to the front of the house wafting the smoke with her feather bundle up the stairwell walls and along the floor as she went. I followed doing the same and, where she turned left at the top of the stairs, I turned right and made my way to the back of the house.

I heard her saying "Cleanse and protect from the darkness" in my room and I started repeating that, too, as I went through the bathroom, the little room across from the kitchen, the kitchen, and then the two back rooms.

I had a strange feeling back there and the cold draft on my neck was disturbing. Mrs. Gray, no doubt. What could I say to her?

"There are some strong energies here these days, Mrs. Gray. Bad ones. I'm sure you know that. We want to purify the house from them, but I don't know what that will do to you. Perhaps it's time for you to move on, too? To be free of us?" I gave her a minute and then I started up saying the "Cleanse and protect" thing, echoing Sunny who was now in her own room.

My bundle went out one time in one of those cold drafts, and I had to relight it with one of my matches to finish off the closets and drawers. When I finished, the cold drafts and the old strange feeling, the sense of a presence, were gone.

Maybe I was going too fast, not being as thorough, but I was done and walking up the hallway to join her when I heard Sunny, still reciting "Cleanse and Protect" as she went into Carl's room. Then, suddenly, it got real quiet.

When she started up again, it was much louder and I picked up my pace and walked into his room in time to see

Sunny waving her smudge stick in front of…Carl?

What was he doing here? I hadn't seen him come in.

He looked angry and Sunny looked determined.

She fanned the smudge stick creating billows of smoke and with the feather bundle directed the smoke up and forward over him. As the smoke flowed over his skin, it seemed to attach itself to him in some way and then to take off tiny bits of him and float away with them. As we watched, his skin, features, bones seemed to fade away and dissipate with the smoke. Like he was being erased or something. Each fresh billow of smoke wafted in to continue the work until he became only a vague image, then a transparency, and finally nothing at all.

All I could say was a whispered, "Wow."

Sunny turned to asked me softly, "Did you see that?"

I nodded and asked, "What the hell just happened?"

"The dark spirit is gone, I think. We've sent it away."

"Carl?"

"Not exactly. Something of…or in him, maybe. It's gone from here now, but…" she shook her head. "What did you find at the back of the house?"

"It felt empty, but I think that was a good thing. I felt a cold breeze a couple of times, and once my bundle went out, but….you know, at the end, I didn't feel Mrs. Gray. Maybe we helped her find a way out."

"Well, that's good, and now we only have a few more things to do."

I retrieved the iron nail and pounded it into the wood at the top of the front door, up above where David usually hung his quotations. It was another protection. Then we lightly scattered the white and gray ashes from the smudge sticks over the front steps. They were there, but not enough that anyone would dirty up our nice clean house by tracking in the dust.

We sat down on the steps again and watched the world go by in companionable silence until, by common consent, we knew it was time to go back in and make sure the smudge sticks and all the candles were out. All that accomplished, we went around closing all the drawers and doors, tidying up.

When Carl came home later, he walked into his room and started cursing.

"What the fuck! My room stinks!"

"We told you we were doing a smudging – that's sage," I said.

"I hate sage! You should have left my room alone, god damn it!"

He threw open the windows and stomped out, leaving us with, "I'm going to stay with Opal until that damn smell is gone!"

Sunny smiled at me. "The purification is working."

"What's going to happen now?"

"I'm not sure, but I think things will get better."

"What was that we saw in Carl's room? We both saw it, but it couldn't have been him."

She only shook her head. "Whatever it was, it's gone now or lost all its power."

CHAPTER THIRTY

The days ticked by and I'd seen no sign that Sally, Elizabeth, Jim, or Carl were going to make their share of the rent. Of course, Carl wasn't really living there anymore. He'd taken some things, left others behind "for the moment," and complained to David that Sunny made him feel unwelcome.

David hadn't nagged or reminded the others about the looming deadline, but Elizabeth and Jim had seen the proverbial handwriting on the wall. After a couple of weeks, they decided to take off, to hitchhike to Oregon, where Jim had some connections. A big snow storm was predicted up there for the day they intended to leave, and Elizabeth was now a shocking shade of yellow. Given her health and the storm, David tried to get them to stay, but they were determined.

Shortly after that Glen sat down with David and said he was splitting. He'd been talking to Lou Gottlieb and was going out to his ranch, the Morning Star, in Sonoma County. It was time for him to get away from city life, he said, and Lou needed help out there. Glen was taking Erin, Star, and Tex with him; he didn't think the Haight was good for any of them, anymore.

We were going to miss them.

I thought all the disruption in the house might really bum Sunny out again, but she seemed to have recovered her good spirits now that David was around more.

Dear Brit,

Thanks for your card and note at Christmas and congratulations on getting into med school! I think you'll be a great doc.

I appreciate your concern, but I'm doing okay. I'll admit that, although things were great here at one time, they aren't now. We've tended to blame the sudden influx last summer of a hundred thousand or so. Picture that many people crowded in an area the size of our old campus. Now add that they had no money for a bed or food. Yeah, it felt sort of like a refugee camp.

As you might imagine, the initial party atmosphere deteriorated rapidly. It got to be more like a Sunday after a college frat house party: the streets were littered with trash; boys slept in doorways; scruffy looking people hung over from days of speeding or shooting up panhandled for 'spare change' on the street; desperate people begged for food; and rumors circulated about thefts, rapes, and guns. Not exactly the Haight I moved into.

I suppose that eventually it would all have broken apart – I mean, how long do most utopian communities last? People have good intentions, but the force of personalities and their histories can easily sabotage things. Let alone laws and regulations.

I don't regret my time here. Quite the contrary: I'm very grateful for it. I really it saved me on a lot of levels.

I'll have to go looking for work soon and for a place to live. That's okay – I've never had a bogeyman mentality about work. I'm only going to trade my time and energy for food and lodging – my soul doesn't come so cheaply. Besides, I don't need that much to live on, and no one can make me do anything I don't want to do.

Granted, any little clerical job I get will help support corporate America, but my not working won't hurt the system one bit.

Besides, maybe it's my karma to be a peon in this life.

And, you know what? I don't care.

I'll do my best and that'll have to be enough. I'll put in my hours, collect a paycheck, and see what I can do about making a good life.

Terry

Carl moved in with Opal permanently and said he'd pick up the rest of his stuff later. That was really no surprise, but they were living in a place LaVey had in the Haight and David said that Carl was dealing drugs full-time now. That would have been okay, too, but he was burning people, giving them meth instead of acid. Not cool, and he was also talking about getting into heroin and cocaine. That was bad news on so many levels, and he certainly was not a role model for me or anyone else.

If I hitched to Oregon, like Elizabeth and Jim, I'd just end up in a place where I didn't know anybody and would probably be in pretty desperate straits. At least when I moved to the Haight, I'd had Sunny to introduce me around.

(And, it didn't snow in California.)

So, here I was, as far as the establishment knew, a druggie hippie with bad credit (I'd skipped on a credit card bill when I dropped out), no job, and soon no place to live. With no place to live, I figured all my stuff (including my precious books and typewriter) would have to go out to the curb.

I still hadn't found out where to have my welfare check sent. I really had to get on that. Ohhh, man…Dropping out had been so easy! Falling back in was another story all together.

What about Leah? Could I put her on the spot and beg for a place to stay? She had a tenant in my old room; I'd have to sleep on her floor, invade her privacy. I supposed that I could dump my stuff and hitch down to LA and stay with Dee. I thought she'd put me up, but it was LA, a bad scene in so many ways.

Not exactly looking good, especially since I wasn't the type who easily asked for help. And the needier I was, the harder it got. I started by deciding that everyone was going to say "no" to me and ended up comatose and paralyzed.

I couldn't promise people that I'd be good for it, for anything they could lend me in the way of a bed or bus money to apply for a job. I wanted to, expected to, but why should they believe me? Me, the druggie hippie who had no respect for mainstream institutions and mores?

No, not sounding good at all.

What was wrong with me, anyway? I kept running around in circles rather than making a decision. Was I waiting for the universe to make one for me? Like I did when I was pregnant? I had to stop that.

Some people thought I was so strong, brave, and decisive. Hah! Little did they know. I mean, just because I threw myself off cliffs – like when I moved west – didn't mean I hadn't dithered around until an event, like the offer of a ride cross country, tipped me over the edge.

At least Zander was back in town from his latest trip. Maybe it was time to do what I'd been saying I would and ask him for a little advice.

Life was cutting my tether to the Haight, and I'd vowed to say "yes." So, where was I?

Let's see…if I wasn't feeding a bunch of people, I might be able to squeak by on my welfare and my cleaning jobs and get a room somewhere. I could try to get more cleaning gigs, but a desk job would pay more and give me a little security. Oh, yes, and benefits.

Would I be selling out to the system, if I went that route?

Some people would think so and I told myself I didn't care, but was it really true? Then I remembered telling David one time that starving was the trap, not work, so maybe it was true.

The straight world didn't have a lot to recommend it these days and hadn't for a while. Vietnam, anti-war and race riots all over the damn place, civil rights demonstrations, marches, people yelling and screaming, throwing things at each other, sometimes shooting, cops rioting… Not a lot of peace and love out there.

But, as I kept telling myself, the Haight I knew was gone and what was left wasn't much. What little there was left seemed to get smaller and smaller with each passing day.

CHAPTER THIRTY-ONE

Sunny bounced into my room with a huge smile on her face. "I was just being stupid about David! He loves me and...ta, da! He's asked me to marry him!"

"Wow," I said. "Far out. What..." but she cut my questions short, sat me down, and told me everything.

There was a lot.

David had been a very busy man.

He had the church all lined up with Father Harris around the corner at All Saints, and they were getting married, going back east, picking up Sunny's kid, Joey, and... The list went on. He'd been putting things in order for all that and hadn't wanted to say anything to Sunny until he was ready.

Holy cow! They were really going to do it.

Kind of a shocker. And now, there was all sorts of stuff she needed to do. Like how much or how little did they want for a wedding? The full deal or only a simple Justice of the Peace thing downtown?

When I was in college, I'd heard girls talking about all the arrangements involved with a wedding, but my only experience had been going to one years ago...and that was in a Jewish temple. I'd never even looked at one of those bride magazines. What kind of help could I be to her?

She must have seen the deer in the headlights look on my face, because she said, "I hope you don't mind, but I'm going to ask Erin to help me out with arrangements and be my Maid of Honor. She's coming back in town next week to help with everything. Glen will take care of Star and then come up for the wedding."

Saved…whew. "Good idea." I said. "I'll be just as happy to help out. Oh, has David picked a Best Man yet?"

"Yes, Earl, and you know what he's giving David as a wedding present? His Buick! (He's getting a new Lincoln – very fancy.) Anyway…we'll have to go over the Buick with a fine-tooth comb to be sure all the drugs are gone, of course. Don't want to get busted on the first week we're married," she laughed. "He'll drop it off day after tomorrow, so don't be surprised to see it out front."

"I'm going to go tell Sally now." She turned as she started out my door, "You're sure you really don't mind about Erin?"

"Oh, very sure. I'd probably have stumbled all over myself. I'll be happy to run errands, trust me."

She gave me a smile and went on her way down the hall to spread the word.

It was good to see her so happy for a change, and I really was happy for her, but…yeah, like now, I was going to have to really, really get serious figuring what to do – and then do it, whatever it was. This kinda nailed it. There would be a date I had to get out of the house and it was coming soon.

I thought again, but only briefly, about finding a room in the Haight, and I still hadn't figured out what to do if I had no address or phone number. I spent two days running around that same old hamster wheel, sliding back into that black pit of mine. Eventually, I decided that if I was going to freak out, I wanted to get there fast, rather than feel myself slowly dragged down and under.

So, I dropped acid one more time.

I swirled into darkness, and then a universe of stars, appeared, bright pin points of light that burned with cold.

I struggled, but I was so tired of fighting; I wanted to get it over with, all of it.

I was scared to death and scared to die; I saw that I always had been.

My life was a constant battle against fear, running or, at best, bluffing my way through.

I was afraid of the emptiness in me, and I wondered if it was in all of us.

I understood that the only way to keep it bearable was to love and be loved.

But I had no one. I constantly fought with myself and warded off others.

That had to change; I couldn't go on this way.

I could die or I could finally learn how to stay and say "yes."

I could die or I could learn to love.

Quite an assignment. I wasn't sure what to do with all that, but I felt like a giant step had been taken and now I needed to prepare myself for opportunities.

Finally, I managed to get together with Zander. Well, actually, Zander and Carol invited me over for dinner at Carol's place, all I had to do was say I'd come.

She had a little one bedroom place near Market and Fillmore. Tiny kitchen, but decent sized living and bed rooms. Not much furniture yet, of course, but she'd picked up chairs and a small table at the wharf, and Zander gave her some of his stuff. She had enough for now and the place felt warm and comfortable.

Big plus: the light was good. Important for any artist, naturally, but it always helped the mood, too.

She made a great batch of spaghetti with a tomato sauce and Italian sausage and served it with a green salad and crusty French bread (and butter). Ahh, the good life.

After we'd eaten our fill and were sitting around over coffee, I finally spit it out.

"I need your advice. The house on Masonic is going to close up, and we all have to leave. Frankly, it's probably just as well. The Haight is going downhill fast, and it's getting kinda dangerous right now.

"Many of the old hippies have left town, gone back to school or work, taken off for the country…I hate to say it, but the people on the streets are mainly those who have nothing to go back to and the people who prey on them.

"I think it's time for me to 'drop in' and get a job, a new place to live, and all that. The thing is, I've only got my welfare check and a couple of cleaning jobs right now. They don't bring in enough for me to get even a small apartment in a safe neighborhood. But, I need a place to live and a mailing address so I can continue getting my welfare check, apply for jobs, and generally get my act together.

"I feel a bit stuck. Is there something I'm not seeing? Do you have any suggestions?"

Zander and Carol looked at each other, and then Zander said, "Funny thing, we knew this was coming and that you'd need a hand.

"We asked you to dinner, not only to see you, but also to tell you that if things get bad, you can stay with us a while, store your stuff at my apartment on Potrero, and crash here. It'll be a little crowded, but no big deal. You could chip in on groceries, yes?"

"Sure. Of course, and do chores and…whatever. You folks would really be saving my ass. I can't thank you enough.

"As for it being crowded, it'll be a hell of a lot better than a doorway someplace."

The plan was for me to live with them until I got a job and put together enough money to get my own place. I figured it would take me about four months to do all that. I'd need to start paying off my debts and sock enough away for an apartment…but I knew a lot about how to live frugally. Maybe I could do it quicker.

Zander and Carol had also started talking about really moving in together, and one idea they'd come up with was that I could take over his apartment lease when I had a job and they found a new place. Neither of their places was big enough for them both, and his lease would be up in five months and Carol had a couple of friends just waiting for her to move out of this one. I'd be doing them a favor and they'd be able to get a bigger place for themselves and the two studios they needed.

Zander's place was a great deal, tiny, yes, but big enough for me and it was really cheap. Amazing really – a fantastic view of the bay. That would be far out for me. And if they got a place close by, I wouldn't feel lonely, and…

But all that was a couple of months away. I needed to think more short-term right then. Like, let's get through the wedding and get me moved and hunting for a job.

Sunny and David were pleased for me and a little relieved, too,

I suspected. Now everyone was pretty much squared away.

I was talking with Sunny about my plans when David got back from his morning studies at the library. The mail had come, and he was waving a letter.

"Look – my Dad has sent us a nice wedding present. This'll help a lot." He handed a check to Sunny whose eyes got big. "$500! Wow! It certainly will."

"Yeah, and listen to what he says," David went on.

> I've enclosed a wedding present for you and Sunny. I figure you'll probably need it.
>
> I'm glad you're coming home, son. Your mother and I have missed you, and, yes, worried about you a lot these past couple of years. Can't say I approve of how you've been living, but every young man seems to need a wild time before settling down.
>
> I wish we'd met your young woman before the wedding and that we could be there, but at least you are getting married, unlike so many these days, and in a real church, too. (We were worried you'd have one of those hippie weddings on a beach or something with a bald man in a yellow robe presiding.)
>
> As for her having a little boy, well, it'll take a bit of getting used to, being instant grandparents, but I reckon we can handle it.
>
> See you soon,
>
> Love,
>
> Mom and Dad
>
> P.S. All our best to Sunny

"That's really cool," said Sunny. "So far, so good, but I wonder what they'll think when they find out I had Joey when I was an unmarried teenager?"

"You don't have to tell them anything, if you don't want to," said David sitting down beside her on the bed. "I've already told them that Joey's father is dead and that you don't like talking about it. Let folks imagine what they want. As soon as I get a job, I'll start the adoption process."

"Will there be any problem with that?" I asked.

"No," said Sunny. "My ex died in Vietnam and his parents never knew Joey was his. He certainly never told them."

"What about your folks? Think they'll give you Joey?"

"Well, they want to meet David before they do, but I think they'll be happy to be free of the responsibility. They aren't exactly the good parent, let alone grand-parent types."

"And your sister, David?" He hadn't mentioned her, and I knew they'd been close.

"Are you kidding? Sue and Mark haven't been able to have any kids – she's going to spoil Joey rotten."

Sunny added, "She actually wrote me a little 'welcome to the family' note."

David put his arm around her, smiled, and said, "Everything is going to be fine."

It sounded like an "and they lived happily ever after" moment, so I smiled, too, nodded, and left it at that.

We'd been waiting for the climate to lighten up in the Haight what with the Death of the Hippie ceremony, the house purification, and the advent of spring with its usual promises, but there hadn't been any miracles. Although… when I thought about it, maybe David and Sunny's marriage was one.

When Erin arrived, she gave me a side-ways look at first, so I jumped in, gave her a hug and a smile, and said, "I am SO glad you're here and are going to be running the show. I'd be clueless. I'll do anything you tell me to."

She gave me a one-arm hug back and we went into the kitchen to make a pot of tea and start planning.

❋

The dress: Erin and Sunny went shopping. It couldn't be the typical white confection, of course. It was going to be a real wedding, yes, but it was still a hippie event. They came back with a really nice white cotton dress with daisies scattered across the fabric.

Flowers were my assignment. Daisies, naturally, woven into a wreath for Sunny's head and gathered in a bouquet for her to carry.

It was kinda fun watching Erin operate. She had everything whipped into shape in nothing flat. Everyone hopped to and was happy to do what was asked. She made the rounds, handing out assignments and praise or words of appreciation.

She caught me watching her and smiling. "Is anything wrong?"

"No. Not in the least. I was just admiring your executive skills. You really handle people well."

She looked a little dubious, wondering if I was being sarcastic, I thought.

"I'm serious – you ever been a manager?" I asked. "You'd be good at it."

She seemed to relax a little at that, said, "Really? Well, okay…in keeping with that, how are the flowers coming along?"

"Great! I'll have them ready. I've been practicing and once I got the knack of it, they were easy."

While we were busy, the groom broke out his one hippie dress-up outfit: a white Nehru jacket, white pants, and some African beads, a number of them bright yellow. Everything was in good shape, and we thought the bride and groom and everybody in the wedding party were going to look good together.

Now, what about food?

Earl was throwing a dinner for the wedding party the night before the event, but that would have to be it. Sunny and David were taking off right after the ceremony in their new car for Santa Cruz and a little honeymoon. (David's Bernal Heights client had lent him his cottage there for the occasion.)

Saturday afternoon and the sun cooperated by shining on the happy couple and keeping the rest of us relatively warm in the dark church.

The Rev was up there in front in his white robes, smiling at us as we made our way down the aisle to find seats in the front rows. Looked like maybe twenty people came, and Zander and Carol sat beside me. The organist played something soothing, while we whispered among ourselves.

When I came in, I noticed Star standing by Glen in the back with David. Glen had bent down and was holding her hand while he talked to her. She looked up at him quite adoringly. Seemed to me like that was all falling nicely into place, too, and I was happy for them.

David and Glen now stood alone in the back waiting

for their cue. They were smiling broadly and shifting their feet nervously.

Finally, the Rev nodded at the organist, and she shifted seamlessly from what she'd been playing into…whatever that piece is for "Here comes the bride…" and David and Earl walked down to take their places in front of the Rev.

Sunny had a death grip on her bouquet, and I could see that she was wondering if this were all a dream as she walked down the aisle. I must say, she looked very…pretty. A nice old-fashioned word that, "pretty."

Arriving at the altar, Sunny and David both struggled a little to be serious, but grins kept breaking through. The Rev smiled at them, put up his hands to quiet the rest of us, and began the rites and all that. They'd opted for the traditional, standard words and Earl and Erin did their jobs of handing over the rings, simple gold bands.

Finally, David was given permission to kiss the bride, and we all applauded and cheered as we followed them out of the church.

Sunny tossed her bouquet, which Erin caught.

We all threw rice, and they were off with a "Just Married" sign on the rear of the car.

Zander, Carol, and I stood around for a few minutes and then we wandered away from the church and got the streetcar home to Carol's place.

When the honeymoon was over, David and Sunny would be back for one afternoon to close up the house before they started the trek back east.

I figured that I'd say my final goodbyes then. That would give me a little more time to get used to things. I was happy for them and all, but sad for myself, missing them already but looking forward to eventually having a place of my own.

So, like a lot of things that year, the sweet was mixed with some sour.

CHAPTER THIRTY-TWO

The final walk through: I wanted to be there for that, too. Saying good-bye to them and to the house.

We met at the door. "The landlord's going to paint the whole place," said David. "All we need to do is be sure that everything is out and the place is locked up.

"I told Carl he could have anything we'd left behind if he cleaned things up. Let's see how he did."

He unlocked the door and we walked up the stairs, our footsteps echoing for the last time on the wooden floors. All the doors were open and you could see down the hall all the way to the windows at the front and the back of the house. It was dead quiet.

"There were still a couple of people here when I moved out," I said. "It's really strange to see it like this."

"It's like it was when I first arrived," said David. "Like we've traveled back in time."

"Like we were never here," added Sunny.

That was a depressing thought, so I said I'd check the back rooms and took off down the hall.

Before I went into the first bedroom, I checked to see if I could feel the old woman. If she was still there I could pay my respects and tell her we were clearing out. I felt nothing; the old girl really seemed to be gone.

A window was open back there, so I closed it. Then, I looked things over, decided it was clean, and took the broom and dustpan leaning against a wall with me when I went into the other room.

There was nothing there either, aside from a couple of small red beads on a shelf and a penny tucked away, hidden in the corner. (A left over from the purification rite, so I didn't move it. Maybe it would be good for the new tenants.)

On to the kitchen where there was a trash can with a lot of dirt and bits and pieces of paper and junk. No food (not even spices) in the pantry or in the refrigerator. I used paper towels that were still there to wipe down the shelves.

The stove needed cleaning, but there weren't any supplies for that.

I joined up with David and Sunny in the front hall, and she handed me a dime-sized diffraction pattern sticker that she'd found in my room. "A reminder of trips taken," she said and I took the token gratefully.

"I found a penny we hid," I told her, "but don't worry: I left it there. And, David, the kitchen...the stove's a bit of a mess and did you really mean to leave the refrigerator?"

"It's okay. I get my damage deposit back in exchange for the refrigerator, and he'll take care of the stove. Remember when we tried to take that refrigerator out of your old apartment?" he asked.

We had a little laugh at that.

"Well," I said, "I closed a window back there and everything else is broom clean. How about up here?"

"It's the same. Broom clean and ready to go," said David. "I'll take that trash can and the broom out to the alley and put them with the other garbage before we lock up."

I took a moment to wander through the front rooms, saying goodbye to my memories, and then followed them down the steps.

Sunny told me the day's plan was to drive east as far as

they could and then put up for the night. They'd be a few
days on the road.

When David got back from the alley, he put the key into
the lock. I heard the key turning and there was something
so final about that sound. It was really over. I knew it just
like I did when the lights came up after a movie.

"Well," he said. "This is it," and he put the key in an
envelope and dropped it through the mail slot. "Thanks for
coming along and helping, Terry."

"There were good times," I said. "Thank you for those
and for all you've both taught me."

"You've been a good friend," said Sunny. "Keep writing
and stay in touch."

"Sure. Safe travels; love you both."

I gave them each a hug and then turned and walked
down to the streetcar stop. At the corner, I looked back and
saw the black Buick cresting the hill.

I felt empty.

CHAPTER THIRTY-THREE

I knew about work, how to fit in with the establishment, how to survive. Like street smarts, I had conventional smarts. I figured I could be a hippie and still have a straight job.

I got a bit of coaching from an employment agency on how to explain my work gap without overtly lying. Short story: I worked my way through school and when I graduated I took a little time off to take trips and see my brother before I settled down to make a career.

Needless to say, I was careful about the language I used in interviews. I could say "cool" every once in a while, but not "groovy," and definitely not "can you dig it?" or, God forbid, "far fucking out."

I thought about that last acid trip often.

The thing about me is that I can stay in denial of my feelings and things around me for a long, long time, but once I've seen the truth, I can't go back. I have to work on problems, fix things, whatever. As in not just "now" but yesterday.

Okay, that's an exaggeration, but that's how it always feels: Imperative.

I may waste a lot of time until I get to that point, but then I make up for it big time.

The funny thing is, I never have any doubt that I'll be

okay in the end.

Yesterday, when I was going to work on the bus, a business man of some sort sat down in the seat next to me. I looked around and saw it was not the only open seat available. He didn't talk to me or anything, just read his paper.

Huh. That was strange, I thought, but I guessed it was okay.

The kicker was the ride home: A young woman sat down in the seat next to me. Again, there were other vacant seats, and when she saw me glance at the books she was carrying, she actually talked to me, asked me if I'd read them.

We had a conversation.

Whatever vibe I used to give off seemed to be gone.

Kind of promising, but also scarier than hell.

Still, I had promised to say "yes" so…

SUMMING UP

Maybe it didn't all start with getting my degree, but that was at least a clear, definitive, and tangible marker. Like I'd been on a highway that ended and led to an off ramp that dumped me in a traffic circle with a confusing array of signs and streets leading into and out of it.

I guess that what I did was pull into a parking area until I could figure things out. Nobody was asking or pushing me to do anything; I just sort of figured I should look for something new.

And, Lord knows, the Haight was new.

What had I wanted?

Something different, I think, at least different from what life had been for me and those around me.

I wanted to, as they liked to say then, expand my consciousness. I wanted to see more possibilities, actualities that I'd been blind to, and I wanted to find answers and solutions.

I didn't want money and status to be the values I worked for, what I aspired to.

I didn't want rage and hate in myself or in the world.

I didn't want to be the person I was expected to be – by my parents or society.

And, what happened to me?

Luckily, nothing dire and ultimately I learned to trust and how to love a bit more freely.

I learned to forgive my own screw-ups and those of others. We're only human, after all, and as the *I Ching* says so often, "No blame."

I came to value the gentle souls, to learn how to let go of anger, hate, and contempt.

I learned to appreciate those who take another path, to realize that differences, even critical ones, can be good and that it is not written that I need to understand everything.

※

Well, at least a little of that. It's all still pretty aspirational, of course.

I have yet to walk on water, but at least I'm no longer drowning.

※

As for the others, what happened to them?

Terry got a Christmas card from Sunny saying that all was well, and Joey liked his new dad.

That was the last she heard from any of them.

NOTES

What is the relationship of this book to reality?

* I lived in a commune on Masonic in the 1967-1968 period.

* I've manipulated reality to tell one small story of that time and place.

* The time and setting are real.

* All names, aside from those of celebrities and other prominent 60s personalities, are fictitious.

* Although some of the characters are based on real people, those presented are often an amalgam of two or more people. Other characters are pure creations.

* Some of the stories, but not all, are based on real events, but may have involved different people or occurred at a different time/place.

* While the author is not the character "Terry," we are close sisters and share many experiences, but nowhere near all.

* Grass: The difference between the grass we smoked in the 60s and that now being sold: the stuff now is much, much stronger. Think of it as the difference between beer and moonshine.

SUSAN KNAPP is the author of *The Album*, a biography/memoir set in 1927 New England that chronicles the childhood sexual abuse of the author's mother, and, writing as S. Z. Knapp, the first two volumes of a projected vampire trilogy: *Red Roses, Bloody Snow* and *Hot Jazz, Cold Blood*. (Volume three expected off press in 2018/19).

Living in the theater-rich town of Ashland, Oregon, she has also authored a one-act play, "The Real Story" and, in a complete departure from form, is working on an illustrated fable (working title "The Raven and Heron").

When not hunched over a keyboard, she spends summers kayaking on the area's many lakes and enjoying the wildlife.

CPSIA information can be obtained
at www.ICGtesting.com
Printed in the USA
FFOW03n1425180917
40110FF